FROGMAN SPY

The Incredible Case of Commander Crabb

By The Same Author
DANGER FROM MOSCOW

COMMANDER CRABB, G.M.

FROGMAN SPY

The Incredible Case of Commander Crabb

J. BERNARD HUTTON

McDowell, Obolensky

New York

Frogman Spy was first published in 1960 by
Neville Spearman Limited, London,
under the title of *Frogman Extraordinary*

© 1960 by J. Bernard Hutton

First Printing

Manufactured in the United States of America by
Quinn & Boden Company, Rahway, N. J.

CONTENTS

ILLUSTRATIONS

FOREWORD

by

PETER J. HUXLEY-BLYTHE*

Frogman Extraordinary † is a unique book. For in addition to giving all the background data to the mysterious disappearance of the wartime hero Lieutenant-Commander Lionel "Buster" Crabb, O.B.E., G.M., R.N.V.R., while diving near the Soviet warships that brought Bulganin and Khrushchev to Britain in 1956, it provides the answers to the numerous questions about what really happened to him.

In the past, authors tackling similar subjects have been forced to rely upon conjecture, rumour and unconfirmed reports that emanate from what can only be described as very unreliable sources.

This is not the case with Mr. Bernard Hutton. He has in his possession a fascinating document that is of the utmost importance to the free world. A top secret Soviet official *dossier* on Commander Crabb that reveals every aspect of the four-year-old enigma.

Those who knew "Crabbie", as I did for many years during and after the war, will easily recognise him from the following pages. The indomitable calm he maintained while labouring under extreme pres-

---

* Peter J. Huxley-Blythe, who served in the Royal Navy during the war in the Atlantic, Mediterranean and Far Eastern theatres of operations, knew Commander Crabb personally. He is Editor of *The Free Russia*, closely linked with the international R.R.F. (Russian Revolutionary Forces) and many other important organisations.

† *Frogman Spy* was first published in London under the title of *Frogman Extraordinary*.

sure at the hands of his captors was quite typical and he must have regretted, as he walked along the prison corridors, that he could not nonchalantly twirl his sword-stick with the crab on the handle as a final act of contempt and defiance.

But that is not all. This is the first time that anyone has had the opportunity of learning how the modern Red inquisitors conduct their interrogations in such notorious Moscow prisons as Lefortovo; how they reduce their victims to a state of submission without inflicting the tortures that were the main characteristic of the Communist State Security service in the earlier days of the Soviet régime.

Had this book appeared prior to the Korean war the British and American military authorities would have been in a position to instruct frontline troops what to expect and how to resist the seductive overtures made by Communist interrogators, should they be unfortunate enough to become prisoners of war. For it must not be forgotten that Eugene Kinhead in his recent book, *In Every War But One*, quoted U.S. Army files to prove that "almost one out of every three (American prisoners of war in Red hands) was guilty of some form of collaboration with the enemy".

Even now, it is not too late for the West to learn from this most important Soviet document the methods and tactics of the highly skilled Red inquisitors. Though the actual *dossier* reached this country not in the original Russian version but in a Moscow-made precise translation, everyone who is familiar with Soviet phraseology will see at first glance that the official translation is a verbatim work.

What is more, the wording in itself proves this is a typical *dossier* from the hidden archives of the Soviet Secret Service.

It is highly probable that the publication of this book will cause yet another Crabb controversy. People will naturally wonder why he agreed to join the Red Navy after resisting all the efforts made to break his resistance and make him confess that he was an Anglo-American spy. As a result, some of them will undoubtedly cry "Treason". And that in itself will give rise to another question, "Is Crabb now a traitor?" In my opinion the only answer can be an emphatic denial of the accusation.

It should be remembered that prior to the outbreak of World War II he had aimlessly wandered the globe. Only when he became a naval officer and a frogman did he find his true *métier*. It was not to last. As a member of the Volunteer Reserve he was duly demobilised early in 1948.

Civilian life proved to be alien to him. The more he saw of it the less he liked it, but the diminishing Royal Navy could find no place for its wartime hero despite his experience. He was only needed in the times of crisis following the loss of H.M. Submarines *Truculent* and *Affray*.

Deprived of his career and his service colleagues Commander Crabb became embittered. He often expressed to me and others the opinion that Britain was being mis-ruled by a clique of Whitehall clerks instead of men who could visualise what the future would demand. And it was in that frame of mind that he was captured by the Red Navy off Portsmouth.

The record shows that in the early days of captivity he forgot his resentment and resumed the status of a naval officer who was determined not to dishonour the country and service he represented.

The Soviets quickly discovered the one chink in his armour, his love of the navy, and they were not to repeat the Admiralty's mistake.

Having observed his behaviour as a prisoner, coupled with full knowledge of his underwater experience, which they could utilise, the Red authorities had no hesitation in offering him the chance to enlist in their own navy.

When first broached on the subject Crabb showed little enthusiasm, and it was only when he was shown that his death had been announced in Britain that he accepted the offer. Surely at that moment his bitterness against what he termed the "rule of Whitehall clerks" must have returned with a vengeance. He was placed in a position where he had nothing to lose and a new naval career to gain.

Therefore, if any recriminations are to be made, perhaps it would be wiser to look nearer home and ascertain who blundered, because if Commander Crabb is useful to the Soviets he could have been of equal or more use to his own country.

However, apart from giving the authentic answer to what in reality happened to Crabb since he mysteriously disappeared, the Soviet secret *dossier* reveals that the Communist spy network here in Britain is more powerful and well-organised than anyone dared to imagine.

Even before Crabb donned his frogman's suit and entered the sea at Portsmouth on April 19, 1956, Admiral Kotov commanding the Soviet ships knew that an attempt was to be made to investigate the secret devices on his flagship's hull. He knew the date this was to be carried out and that Crabb was to be the frogman. This information, classified "Top Secret", had been relayed to him by a member of a Communist spy ring. . . .

And finally, as we read this remarkable book we find that one axiom of the lurid spy-thrillers is indeed true to life. That when a spy is caught, irrespective of who and how brave he might be, he is disowned without any compunction. Tragic yet necessary.

Fleetwood.
March 1960

I

ATTEMPTS AT SOLVING THE MYSTERY

Commander Lionel Kenneth Philip Crabb, O.B.E., G.M., R.N.V.R., disappeared mysteriously in Portsmouth Harbour on April 19, 1956—a day after the Russian warships, which had brought Marshal Bulganin and Mr. Khrushchev to England, lay at anchor in Stokes Bay. His friends made every possible attempt to find out what had happened to him. But as he was in the R.N.V.R. Special Branch, and was employed as a civilian diver by the Admiralty Research Laboratory at Teddington, the Navy clamped down on news of the death. All that a friend of his managed to get out of the Admiralty was the short answer: "He is dead." And the police, who normally would have been told of a death by drowning, knew nothing.

It was not before April 29 that the Admiralty— forced by spreading rumours and direct inquiries about Commander Crabb's fate—made the following short announcement:

"He is presumed to be dead as a result of trials with certain underwater apparatus. The location was in Stokes Bay, and it is nine days since the accident."

Next morning great publicity was given to the mystery of the "Naval hero, holder of the George

Medal, won as one of Britain's first frogmen". It was also stated in the press that:

Admiralty officials said last night that he had not been diving under the Russian ships to investigate their propellers and hull forms. The Russians often had their divers down during their stay. This is normal procedure: our Navy does the same with its ships, when in harbour.

The "Crabb Mystery" became a nation-wide affair. Not only the newspapers but also scores of other investigators did their level best to find out what had actually happened to the 46-year-old, 5 ft. 5 in. frogman hero. Consequently, on May 3, 1956, a *Daily Telegraph* reporter was able to reveal that Commander Crabb had been staying at the Sallyport Hotel, a small residential hotel in Portsmouth High Street, and that:

Two days after Crabb's disappearance Det.-Supt. Stanley Lamport, Chief of Portsmouth C.I.D., called at the hotel and removed four pages from the register covering the first three weeks in April. He signed the next page as a receipt. Cdr. Crabb never returned to the hotel and the servants were warned not to say anything about his movements. Last night the proprietor, Mr. Edward Richman . . . refused to discuss the matter. He said it was not uncommon for the police to act in such a way. . . .

The same morning *The Times* published the following:

It was established that on April 21 Detective Superintendent Jack Lamport, head of Portsmouth C.I.D., removed four pages from the register of the Sallyport Hotel in High Street, Old Portsmouth. It is assumed that this was done because the pages contained the signatures of Commander Lionel Crabb, whom the Admiralty "presumed dead". . . .

The Portsmouth Police said tonight that the matter was finished as far as they were concerned.

On inquiry at the Admiralty *The Times* was told: "We have no information of any kind."

The *Evening Standard* reporter was told at the Gosport headquarters of the Navy's frogmen on May 3, 1956:

There were no rescue attempts by us on April 20. Lieut.-Commander Crabb was not employed by us.

The *Evening Standard* reporter also stated that on May 3 an Admiralty spokesman denied that Commander Crabb's work had anything to do with the Russian warships and, to his inquiries about the removal of four pages from the Sallyport Hotel register by Supt. S. J. Lamport, the police spokesman said that Supt. Lamport had been acting "on instructions from a higher authority than us".

Meanwhile, the following rumours and theories were circulating amongst the population:

1. Commander Crabb was killed by the Russians, who mistook him for a saboteur, operating under the keel of the cruiser *Ordzhonikidze* in Portsmouth Harbour. His body was found floating in the water, and the frogman was secretly buried at midnight in the cemetery, with full military honours.

2. Crabb is alive. He was captured by the Russians, kept a secret prisoner in the cruiser and taken back to Russia.

3. He was forced to the surface near the Russian ships by failure of his oxygen breathing apparatus. Captured and taken back to Russia as a suspected spy.

4. Frogman Crabb was carrying some submarine equivalent of a fountain-pen size geiger instrument, which would detect any atom bomb hidden in the underwater magazines of the Russian ships.

5. Commander Crabb was trapped by the cable of a portable TV camera when he was photographing the bottom of the Russian cruiser.

6. It's all a sensational publicity stunt that went wrong.

Because these rumours and theories were circulating, not only in Portsmouth itself but were spreading all over the country, the Admiralty and political authorities conferred as to whether to issue an official statement. But they decided against this, and the Admiralty consequently added nothing to its previous announcement, nor did it confirm or deny anything.

Determined attempts to solve the mystery were made untiringly. On May 4, 1956, the *Daily Telegraph* wrote:

It is possible that Cdr. Lionel Crabb, the George Medal frogman, was engaged in secret work when he died. . . .
No one in Portsmouth knows whether Cdr. Crabb was working for an intelligence organisation, possibly checking on the Asdic apparatus underneath the Russian cruiser *Ordzhonikidze*, 12,000 tons, resulting in his death as he tried to reach the bottom. . . .
The possibility that Russian divers engaged on checking underneath the cruiser at regular intervals discovered Cdr. Crabb's body has not been overlooked. Until it is found no inquest can be held. So far no attempt has been made by the Naval authorities to find his body. It could have been swept out to sea.
On April 19, Cdr. Crabb is believed to have gone to a

spot near Gosport ferry and entered the water wearing diving equipment. But where he went from there is not known.

If he did not wish to be detected on his mission he could have used oxygen breathing gear. This does not send up tell-tale air bubbles directly above, but it is dangerous to use in depths over 30 feet.

The draught of the Russian cruiser would be about 33 feet. If air breathing sets are used the depth a diver can reach safely does not arise.

From inquiries made after Cdr. Crabb left London on April 17, I learn that he arrived the same day at the Sally-port Hotel, Portsmouth, with another fair-haired man considerably younger than himself. They booked two rooms.

The following morning Cdr. Crabb left alone before the hotel staff came on duty. He returned in the evening.

On Thursday morning, April 19, he again left early. The man with him, who had signed the register in the name of "Matthew Smith", came down later, paying the hotel bill in cash for both.

The Admiralty have admitted that Cdr. Crabb was working for them, but have not disclosed to which branch he was attached. It is unlikely that at 46 he was working directly for the Navy on such exhausting diving work.

But it is possible that after leaving the Service a year ago he was approached by a secret unit working under the direction of the Admiralty and asked to do special underwater work if called upon.

The possibility that he was engaged on some secret work is strengthened by the fact that no one was with him when he entered the water. It can only be assumed that after he failed to return to an appointed rendezvous on April 19 the man who was with him informed the Admiralty that he was overdue.

I learned yesterday that six months ago, when two Russian cruisers and four destroyers were berthed at Portsmouth, Cdr. Crabb visited the dockyard area.

Next day, May 5, 1956, *The Times* wrote the following:

The mystery of the death of Commander Lionel Crabb, one of the first of the Royal Navy's wartime frogmen, was deepened last night by a report that an assistant Naval attaché at the Soviet Embassy in London had said that a watchman in the Soviet cruiser *Ordzhonikidze* had seen a frogman near the ship when it was at Portsmouth. The report stated that the frogman had surfaced for a few seconds and then disappeared.

Captain N. P. Eliseenko, Naval Attaché at the Soviet Embassy, refused to comment on the report when questioned by a representative of *The Times*. Another official commented: "Commander Crabb was an English frogman, not a Russian. Therefore we cannot say anything. It is a matter for your Admiralty."

At the Admiralty it was stated: "We have no comments or observations to make."

Official reticence about the activities which led to the death of Commander Crabb has caused much speculation. The theory that is most persistently advanced is that he was having a close look at the Russian ships which brought the Soviet leaders to this country on April 18. . . .

Mr. Marshall Pugh, who is writing a biography of Commander Crabb, said yesterday that the suggestion has been made in the newspapers that Commander Crabb was not engaged in national work at the time of his death. "I should like to point out," said Mr. Pugh, "that a senior Naval officer first confirmed to Commander Crabb's mother and his associates, including myself, that Commander Crabb was missing. He made it clear to all of us that Commander Crabb had died on service."

The *Daily Express* told its readers the same morning:

A frogman was spotted in Portsmouth Harbour by a

lookout in the B and K cruiser, the Russians said yesterday. The question is: Was that frogman Lieut.-Commander Lionel (Buster) Crabb?

The paper also revealed that a Soviet Assistant Naval Attaché told the *Evening Standard* Naval reporter Gordon Holman:

"A watchman in our ship saw a frogman come to the surface.

"He was on the surface for only a few seconds. Then he disappeared and was not seen again.

"The watchman reported to the captain of the warship."

Asking whether any action was taken against the frogman, Mr. Holman received the following reply from the Soviet Assistant Naval Attaché: "Absolutely none. We are in a British port and there was nothing we could do." He said that he did not know on which day the frogman was seen, that the captain did not report the incident to London, and that the information had just arrived from Moscow.

The *Daily Express* deepened the Commander Crabb mystery by disclosing that at Portsmouth Captain John Grant, commanding officer of H.M.S. *Vernon,* the establishment that houses the Naval diving school, said:

"If a frogman was seen near the Russian cruiser he certainly did not come from here."

The *Daily Express* then asks these questions:

What *did* happen to Commander Crabb? Was he drowned by accident? Killed trying to get a close-up of that cruiser underwater? Captured by the Russians?

Investigations to get to the bottom of it all continued in full swing.

On May 6, 1956, the *Empire News* expressed the opinion that Commander Crabb "was killed in an attempt to ensure the safety of the Soviet cruiser *Ordzhonikidze* after threats that fanatical refugee ex-sailors in Britain were plotting to attach a limpet mine to its hull". This opinion was based on an interview between an *Empire News* reporter and Rear-Admiral George P. Thomson, submarine expert and wartime press censor, who told the reporter:

"I cannot say if any actual threat was made, but the Naval Authorities' responsibility for visiting cruisers' safety were in duty bound to take every precaution.

"The possibility of a daring frogman attaching a limpet mine to the hull of the ship was a security risk that had to be guarded against in common with other risks.

"It was the Navy's obvious duty to guard against even the possibility of such an attempt. Even I have not been told what happened and there may be very sound reasons for never disclosing exactly how Commander Crabb was reported missing.

"Two facts seem most significant. The Admiralty have confirmed that Crabb was taking part in underwater experiments in the vicinity, and the Russians, when asked, made no secret of seeing a frogman near their ships.

"If Crabb had been ordered to carry out an underwater search in the interests of the Russians' security it would, of course, have been absolutely necessary to observe the utmost secrecy.

"It is almost certain that the Russians made their own underwater searches, which is normal practice, and if we double-checked, it might not be advisable to tell them.

"Our motives might not have been fully understood."

The *Sunday Dispatch*, reconstructing on May 6, 1956, the facts so far known about Commander

Crabb, disclosed that the proprietor of the Sallyport Hotel explained Superintendent Lamport's removal from the hotel register of the four pages which included the names of Crabb and his friend by saying: "So no outsider can trace who might have talked to them." Adding the hotel proprietor's opinion: "I do not think Commander Crabb is dead," the *Sunday Dispatch* went on:

Others close to the 46-year-old monocled commander, who carried a swordstick with a crab handle, also believe he is alive.

His wife, from whom he was separated 18 months ago, Mrs. Margaret Elaine Crabb, and the housekeeper of the flats where Crabb lived, feel he is not dead.

Commenting last night on the theory that Commander Crabb was accidentally drowned while inspecting the Russian cruiser's hull as a security check against saboteurs, Rear-Admiral George P. Thomson, submarine expert and chief wartime censor, said:

"IN VIEW OF THE FACTS KNOWN, AND FROM THE POINT OF VIEW OF INTERNATIONAL RELATIONS, IT IS THE BEST POSSIBLE SOLUTION TO A PROBLEM OF THIS KIND.

"I can assure you, I know nothing more than you—nobody does."

But if he had drowned his body should have floated to the surface by now.

No search of the harbour has been made at any time.

The night the Russian cruiser arrived, floodlights over the stern covered the water where a frogman would be if he were trying to inspect the cruiser's screws that are said to drive her at a phenomenal speed. By day Russian divers were seen round the ship.

Many of Commander Crabb's friends in Portsmouth say he discovered too much about the cruiser and was kidnapped. . . .

So the strenuous efforts to solve the riddle went on.

On May 7, 1956, the *Daily Express* asked the question which the whole British nation was—and is—interested in: WHO WAS FROGMAN CRABB WORKING FOR? and went on to say the following:

First truths in the incredible frogman blunder emerged yesterday. They are:

Frogman Lionel (Buster) Crabb DID go out to the Red cruiser which brought B and K to Portsmouth and:

The Admiralty DID NOT know until Lieutenant-Commander Crabb, a demobilised Special Volunteer Reservist, was presumed dead.

It is now clear that the First Lord of the Admiralty, Lord Cilcennin; the Director of Naval Intelligence, Rear-Admiral John G. T. Inglis; and the Commander-in-Chief of the Fleet, Sir George Creasy, were not told.

And now it is said that the Admiralty Board, had it known, would not have approved because of:

1. The risk of imperilling political relationships with the Soviets during the B and K talks with the Prime Minister.

2. The risk to any diver's life by sending him on a hazardous single-handed underwater reconnaissance of the Russian warship.

Security, Foreign Office, and Admiralty officials held a special meeting to decide whether a statement should be issued.

Admiralty chiefs were in favour of making a statement to allay public curiosity and end rumours. They were forbidden to do so.

This veto is likely to be challenged in the Commons on Wednesday.

The same morning the *Daily Mail* revealed the following sensation:

For 48 hours now Sydney Knowles, 34-year-old frogman, has searched Portsmouth Harbour, trying to find out what happened to his best friend, Commander Lionel ("Buster") Crabb. . . .

Sydney last night identified the mystery "Mr. Smith" who stayed with Crabb in Portsmouth's Sallyport Hotel on April 16 and 17.

He found an old friend who said that with his wife they spent the evening of April 17 with Buster and someone introduced as "Lofty".

The description they gave—tall, slim and fair-haired, with a Scottish accent and a cultured voice—tallied with that of "Mr. Smith" given by the hotel manager.

Though he says he knows for a fact that Buster was asked to inspect the Russian cruiser *Sverdlov* last year, Sydney does not think the Admiralty would call him back to do the same thing again.

But he intends to find out what really did happen. And last night Buster's mother rang him up from her Oxfordshire home to thank him for trying.

Next day the *Daily Mail* was able to say more of what Commander Crabb's best friend experienced while attempting to find out whatever he could. The article, entitled "I KNOW WHAT CRABB DID", states:

Just before midnight Mr. Sydney Knowles, 34, who fought beside frogman Crabb during the last war, prepared to dive into Portsmouth Harbour to search for him. "I shall never rest happy until I find Buster Crabb's grave," he said.

But a short time before he planned to enter the water a serving officer approached him and said: "Don't dive —'Crabbie' is not there."

The officer claimed that he knew exactly what happened to frogman Crabb on the secret mission he began on the day a Russian cruiser came into the harbour here.

"I know an awful lot about this," said the officer, a

friend of Mr. Knowles, "but I am sworn under the Official
Secrets Act not to say anything.

"I heard of your attempt to find Buster. It is a hazardous
mission and I came here to stop you doing it because I
would hate to see any friend of mine or Buster sticking
his neck out when I know there was nothing to gain.

"I know Buster's not down there—don't ask me why
but I just do."

So Mr. Knowles abandoned his dive. He said: "My
officer friend and every diver I have met in the diving
school at H.M.S. *Vernon* here are convinced that
'Crabbie' is still alive. I have a feeling that he's still alive
and is being hidden by the organisation that sent him to
dive. It's just supposition. . . ."

Other newspapermen were, however, more in
favour of the theory that Commander Crabb was
dead. On May 8, 1956, the *Daily Express*, for instance,
considered the following possibility:

Frogman Lionel (Buster) Crabb may have been
ELECTROCUTED underwater while trying to take
pictures of the B and K cruiser at Portsmouth. . . .

A storm broke loose when Prime Minister Sir
Anthony Eden made a short statement about Commander Crabb's death in Parliament on May 9, 1956.
Next morning *The Times* gave the following
information about what had taken place:

A fruitless Opposition attempt was made yesterday to
get the Speaker's permission to move the adjournment of
the House, after the Prime Minister had steadily refused
to enlarge on his short statement about the death of Commander Lionel Crabb, the frogman who was reported
missing after a dive in Stokes Bay, near Portsmouth
Harbour, on April 19.

Although Labour members received with sounds of

shocked surprise Sir Anthony Eden's decision, in the public interest, not to disclose the circumstances in which Commander Crabb was presumed to have met his death, the House heard in almost complete silence the news that what had been done was without the authority or knowledge of Ministers and that appropriate disciplinary steps were being taken.

The Prime Minister's firm refusal to be drawn by taunts of evasion and the like was warmly applauded from the benches behind him, but the Opposition showed themselves increasingly restive at his resistance to their pressure for more information.

The subject arose on Mr. J. Dugdale's question asking for the evidence on which the Admiralty officially presumed the death of Commander Crabb; what were the circumstances of his disappearance; and whether efforts were still being made to locate the body.

Sir Anthony Eden replied: "It would not be in the public interest—(Opposition cries of Oh!)—to disclose the circumstances in which Commander Crabb is presumed to have met his death. While it is the practice for Ministers to accept responsibility, I think it is necessary, in the special circumstances of this case, to make it clear that what was done was done without the authority or the knowledge of Her Majesty's Ministers. Appropriate disciplinary steps are being taken."

Mr. Dugdale said this was one of the most extraordinary statements ever made by a Prime Minister. It was a complete evasion of Ministerial responsibility. Mr. Dugdale then put these questions:

Why was Commander Crabb diving in the close vicinity of the Soviet cruiser here on a friendly visit? Under whose authority was a police officer sent to the hotel at which Commander Crabb was staying with another man, ordering the leaves of the register showing their names to be torn out? What was the name of the other man? Why did the police officer threaten the hotel proprietor with the Official Secrets Act?

The Prime Minister replied: "I thought it right to make the statement which I have made, and I have nothing to add to it." (Ministerial cheers.)

Mr. Gaitskell, leader of the Opposition, said: "The Prime Minister will be aware that a great deal of information has already been published in the press. Does he not think on reflection, in view of the amount of speculation which undoubtedly will continue in the absence of any information from the Government, that it really would be wiser in the general interest, if a fuller explanation were given?" (Opposition cheers.)

Sir Anthony Eden replied that he had given the fullest consideration to this matter. "I can assure Mr. Gaitskell," he went on, "that there are certain issues which are the responsibility of the Prime Minister himself, and having given all reflection to all the information at our disposal I thought it my duty to give the answer I have, and I am afraid I must tell the House that I cannot vary from the answer."

Describing the answer as "totally unsatisfactory to the Opposition", Mr. Gaitskell asked: "Is the Prime Minister aware that while we would all wish to protect public security, suspicion must inevitably arise, that his refusal to make a statement is not so much in the interest of public security as to hide a very grave blunder which has occurred?"

The Prime Minister rejoined that the House and the country "must draw their conclusions from what I have said [Opposition cries of 'It will!'], and also from what I declined to say.

"Mr. Gaitskell," he went on, "will understand I have weighed up these considerations and they have weighed heavily in my answer. With his experience he knows there are some of these decisions only a Prime Minister can take, and I am convinced after the most careful reflection the decision was the right and only one."

Mr. Gaitskell then asked: "Are we to take it, in the absence of any further statement from the Prime

Minister, and, in the light of what he has just said about the public drawing their own conclusions, that in fact officers or an officer of Her Majesty's Forces was engaged upon the business of espionage during the Russian visit?"

Sir Anthony Eden: "Mr. Gaitskell is perfectly entitled to put any wording he likes on what I said. My words stand as they are without any gloss anyone can put on them."

Replying to Mr. Shinwell, who asked against whom the Prime Minister was taking disciplinary action, and for what reason, Sir Anthony Eden said: "What I said was that disciplinary steps are being taken."

Mr. Shinwell asked if action was to be taken against some individual or individuals who gave instructions to Commander Crabb; and if it was because they defied authority, or because they acted without consulting Ministers. The Prime Minister repeated: "I have nothing to add to my answer."

Mr. Dugdale sought leave to move the adjournment of the House, in view of the Government's failure to give a satisfactory explanation of the events connected with the disappearance of Commander Crabb.

The Speaker, giving his ruling, said: "This application is governed by authority. When a Minister refuses to answer a question on the grounds of public interest it has been ruled in the past—and I adhere to it—that that is a matter which cannot be raised, and therefore I must decline the application. . . ."

Apart from having reported the debate in Parliament in full, *The Times* also revealed that when the Admiralty was asked whether the statement about Commander Crabb's death was still as announced on April 29, 1956, the Chief of Naval Information, Captain A. W. Clarke, said:

"The Admiralty has no comment, no further information, and is not prepared to answer any questions at all. . . ."

A Naval spokesman at Portsmouth said, on the question of disciplinary steps: "I have no knowledge of anything in this connection in the Portsmouth Command." A similar statement was made at H.M.S. *Vernon*, the Navy's underwater establishment at Portsmouth.

The great mystery deepened. All sorts of rumours and theories swept the country, but no true light was really thrown upon the riddle which was on everyone's mind. Then, on May 12, 1956, *The Times* published the following addition:

The Soviet Government announced that it had sent a Note to Britain stating that Russian sailors on board the cruiser *Ordzhonikidze*, which brought Mr. Bulganin and Mr. Khrushchev to Britain, saw a frogman approach the vessel while she was in Portsmouth Harbour. Moscow radio, which broadcast the text of the Soviet Note, also quoted a British Note in reply. This Note, it is said, expressed regret and said that the frogman's activities were carried out without the permission of the British Government.

The radio said that the Soviet Note was delivered on May 4, and that the British reply arrived on May 9. The Note from the Soviet Embassy said:

"During the stay of Soviet warships in Portsmouth, at 7.30 a.m. on April 19 seamen on board the Soviet ship observed a frogman floating between the Soviet destroyers. The frogman, who wore a black diving suit with flippers on his feet, was seen on the surface of the water for one to three minutes, and then dived again alongside the destroyer *Smotriashchin*.

"The commanding officer of the Soviet ships, Rear-Admiral Kotov, in a conversation with the Chief of Staff of the Portsmouth Naval base, Rear-Admiral Burnett, drew his attention to the case. Rear-Admiral Burnett categorically rejected the possibility of the appearance of a frogman alongside the Soviet ships, and stated that at the time indicated there were no operations in the port involving the use of frogmen. In actual fact, however, as it transpired from reports published in the British press on April 30, the fact that the British Naval Authorities had carried out secret underwater tests in the area where the Soviet warships were anchored at Portsmouth was confirmed. Moreover, these tests resulted in the death of the British frogman.

"It is sufficient to recall that the newspaper *Daily Sketch,* in a brief article on the end of frogman Crabb, reported the following: He dived for the last time in Stokes Bay, at the spot of secret diving operations near the anchorage of the Soviet ship *Ordzhonikidze.*

"Attaching great importance to such an unusual fact as the carrying out of secret frogman tests alongside Soviet ships on a friendly visit in the British Naval base of Portsmouth, the Embassy would be grateful to the British Foreign Office for an explanation on this matter."

The Times also revealed the text of the British Note in reply, as quoted by Tass in Russian as follows:

"As has already been publicly reported, Commander Crabb carried out frogman tests, and, as is assumed, lost his life during these tests. The frogman who, as reported in the Soviet Note, was discovered from the Soviet ships swimming between the Soviet destroyers, was in all appearances Commander Crabb. His presence in the vicinity of the destroyers occurred without any permission whatever, and Her Majesty's Government express their regret for the incident."

The Times also published a report from its Moscow correspondent, saying:

Official Soviet publications took cognizance today for the first time of the case of Commander Crabb, but shed no new light on the mystery. Whatever knowledge the Russians may or may not have of what took place underwater in Stokes Bay during the visit of the cruiser *Ordzhonikidze,* or of what happened to Commander Crabb's body, no information on either question was offered by the Government newspaper *Izvestia* or by the Communist Party's *Pravda,* which published accounts of the case.

Both newspapers indicated acceptance of Sir Anthony Eden's explanation in the House of Commons that the frogman's activities were carried on without the knowledge or authority of the British Government. Accounts by the respective newspapers' correspondents in London referred to the episode as an attempt at "underwater espionage".

There is no doubting the tone of indignation in *Pravda* and *Izvestia. Pravda* called it a "shameful operation of underwater espionage directed against those who came to England on a friendly visit".

In concluding its account *Izvestia* offered this comment: "Pressure of public opinion in Britain has brought to light of day the sordid doings of the adversaries of international co-operation and closer understanding among peoples. There need be no doubt that the British people will be able to defend their vital interests from the intrigues of those few, but, as life shows, still far from harmless circles."

On May 13, 1956, the *Sunday Times,* writing of the exchange of Notes between Britain and Russia on the activities of Commander Crabb, and stating that "a Foreign Office spokesman declined to accept the description of the Soviet action as a 'breach of confidence' but conceded that it was a breach of manners", raised this interesting question:

Did Marshal Bulganin know all about the incident before he left Britain? At the farewell press conference he said: "The course of the discussions met on their way certain underwater rocks." Portsmouth rocks?

On May 13, 1956, the *News of the World* managed to publish an article by Mr. Arthur Tomkins, Commander Crabb's friend for over 30 years, who wrote:

I believe I am the last man with whom Buster Crabb talked in London before he went on his fateful and fatal mission. . . .
When he did not appear next day we thought little of it, but the day after I rang an old diving friend who said he would get in touch with the Admiralty. We heard no more.
Then we contacted one or two of his other diving friends, but no one knew anything. Finally I rang the Admiralty. There I was told: "He has failed to resurface after a dive, but don't worry for a day or two."
Again we rang, this time to be told he had entered the water to test new diving gear and that the Admiralty intended to make an announcement to that effect. But later the same day I was told that no statement would be made. And none was made until a week after Buster's disappearance.

Mr. Zilliacus, Labour M.P. for Gorton, Manchester, made a speech on May 13, 1956, in Nottingham, during which he said:
"I believe that the Prime Minister, as he said in the House of Commons last week, really did not authorise Commander Crabb's activities on this occasion. The

most likely explanation is the possibility that Commander Crabb, who had retired but was still taken on from time to time for special jobs, had on this occasion been employed by the United States Secret Service with the complicity of their and his contacts in the British Secret Service."

On May 14, 1956, the Parliamentary Correspondent of *The Times* reported the following:

The Prime Minister tonight ended his short speech on the case of Commander Crabb, the frogman, by deploring the debate raised by the Opposition and he was rewarded by a long, loud cheer from the benches behind him. From the Opposition came a low growl of dissatisfaction, which carried some cries of "resign". . . .

To mark their disapproval of this "misconceived and inept operation", and in protest against the Prime Minister's refusal to answer any of their questions, Mr. Gaitskell tonight moved the reduction of the token vote on which the debate was held. The motion was negatived by 316 votes to 229.

The Prime Minister refused to amplify his statement of last Wednesday though he explained the reasons for what he had not said then. He based his attitude on the national interest of security, but in a sudden quiet passage at the end he invoked also the international interest.

With great vehemence he said that all he cared for was that the outcome of the discussions with the Soviet leaders should, in truth, prove to be the beginning of the beginning. "I intend to safeguard that possibility at all costs," he declared. "I believe it is also in the minds of the Soviet leaders. It is for that reason that I deplore this debate and will say no more."

His earlier words in a crowded, expectant House with the First Lord of the Admiralty and the First Sea Lord up in the Peers' Gallery, and Sir Winston Churchill an attentive listener below, were in firm defence of his reticence. He told the House bluntly that they were dealing with circumstances in which no government in any country would say more than he was prepared to say.

This warning reduced the House to silence. The Prime Minister explained that there was nothing contrary to Parliamentary practice in his attitude and there was no dispute about the general principle that there were certain things which it was against the national interest to disclose. He recalled that Mr. Gaitskell had spoken very freely about the secret service and had speculated about their control, organisation and efficiency.

Sir Anthony Eden said he was not prepared—and he apologised for having to say it—to discuss these matters in the House. He reflected that it was easy for Mr. Gaitskell to imply that all was not well. "I could not answer," he said, "because I could not answer him generally or in detail without disclosing matters which, as he recognises, must remain secret."

It had never been the practice to discuss these matters openly in the House. "I am not prepared to break that precedent," said the Prime Minister. He insisted that it must be left to the discretion of Ministers to decide these matters. A Minister could not disclose the reasons for his decisions. If he did he would be disclosing what he judged was contrary to the public interest. That was the position in this matter.

With great deliberation, a pause between each word, the Prime Minister said: "Therefore on this aspect of the matter I must tell the House now I have not one word more to say than I announced on Wednesday." The Government side raised a subdued cheer and the Opposition murmuring bore some cries of "Shame".

Sir Anthony Eden explained the exceptional course he took on Wednesday of making it plain that what was done was without the authority of Ministers, and he made it clear that that included all Ministers and all aspects of the affair.

He felt it necessary also to let it be known that

disciplinary steps were being taken. It showed that the Government were determined that the proper measure of control and authority should be exercised by Ministers in all matters of this kind.

The only other matter which the Prime Minister dealt with was the fact that he did not inform the House on Wednesday of the Government's receipt of the Russian Note and their reply to it. He denied that he had been holding back information which the House should have had. The Soviet Note was delivered to the Foreign Office on Friday night and in the Foreign Secretary's absence he approved the answer to it on Wednesday morning.

He claimed also that there was nothing inconsistent in that reply and his statement to the House on Wednesday. He realised that the Soviet Government might publish both the Note and the reply, but even so it would not have been possible for him to communicate either the effect or text of the Note in advance of the reply being received.

Mr. Gaitskell had combined in his opening speech a measure of restraint and care for security with an effect of probing for the truth. He based it on the constitutional principle that a Minister should take responsibility for what had happened and he deduced that other departments, apart from the secret service, appeared to have been involved. But nobody, he said, could claim that these operations were successfully secret and there had been some embarrassment to foreign relations.

He fully accepted the Prime Minister's disclaimer of ministerial knowledge or approval and said that it should be accepted by the Soviet Government as well as complete evidence of good faith. He did not believe that this episode would do permanent damage to our relations with the Soviet Government, who were realists in this matter.

He was more concerned with what appeared to be the situation in the secret service, because what had been suggested by the Prime Minister's original statement revealed a very grave lack of control at home and a most unsatisfactory state of affairs within the service.

Presumably the secret service and the Admiralty must have been mixed up in the plan from the start. An extraordinary feature of the whole business was the question of how Commander Crabb approached the Soviet vessels if it was the Admiralty's responsibility to guard them.

Referring to the reported episode of the removal of pages from a hotel register, Mr. Gaitskell said it was hard to see by what right the police officers made the hotel keeper break the law. It was a matter of great importance that the secret service should not be above the law.

Mr. Gaitskell concluded that it was impossible for the nation to pass final judgment, but an impression had been created of a most deplorable lack of co-ordination and control between the Foreign Office, the secret service, and the Admiralty, and an impression of unusual technical incompetence.

Among the back-bench speakers a Conservative, Lieutenant-Colonel Cordeaux, said it would be wrong for the House to lose faith in the secret service because of this case, but it was impossible to excuse it. It was approved as mistakenly and rashly as it was ineptly carried out and he felt alarmed for the higher direction of whatever service might be concerned. Commander Crabb was of an age when he should hardly have been chosen for such a hazardous operation. But Lieutenant-Colonel Cordeaux was convinced that the Russians would attach very little importance to this episode.

The Parliamentary debate on May 14, 1956, by no means put an end to the efforts which newspapermen and others made to try to solve the deepening mystery of what was really behind the Commander Crabb affair. On May 16, 1956, the *Daily Mail* published an article by Marshall Pugh, which read:

Two significant items are missing from the clothing

and personal possessions which Commander Crabb left in his hotel room before his last dive into Portsmouth Harbour. They are his swordstick and his wallet. These are the only two things which have not been returned to his mother.

The swordstick was one of Crabb's most treasured belongings. It was about 3 ft. in length; the case of black, silver-tipped ebony, the handle engraved with a golden crab.

It was presented by a friend in Spain, and Crabb carried it on all his missions to Portsmouth—including the last one.

The missing wallet may have contained the 60 guineas which his business associates believe he was to be paid for the underwater job.

Some time during the last week the naval captain who had first informed Commander Crabb's mother that her son was missing called on her again at her Oxfordshire home.

With him he brought the suitcase which Commander Crabb had left in the Sallyport Hotel . . . the suitcase which disappeared with the mysterious Mr. Bernard Smith who returned to the Sallyport to pay the bill.

But there was no sign of the wallet or the swordstick.

Mrs. Crabb had no wish to embarrass the authorities. She said nothing.

But on Friday, May 11, Crabb's business associates sent a personal letter to the captain who returned the gear. They pointed out that the wallet and "another valued possession" was missing. The captain has not replied.

A pork-pie hat, an eye-glass in the top left waistcoat pocket, and the swordstick were all part of "Crabbie's" almost ceremonial dress on his frequent "little jobs down in Portsmouth".

There was also a ceremonial joke. When his naval diving friends at H.M.S. *Vernon*, who suspected that he was involved in Secret Service work, saw him in that dress they would say: "Hullo, Crabbie. Something on?" And he would reply: "Just dropped in for a shave and a haircut."

A Portsmouth knave might have stolen Crabb's wallet, but only a very foolish knave would have stolen Crabb's stick. For it would be recognised by almost every clearance diving officer in the Royal Navy.

The British public all over the country was most interested in what was at the bottom of the Commander Crabb mystery, and people discussed the case at every opportunity. Fantastic rumours were spread about him, and the most widespread ones were still:

That he had been accidentally killed by the Russians when they found him inspecting the hull of the cruiser to make sure no one had mined it;

Kidnapped because he had discovered too much about the ship's equipment;

Drowned and secretly buried with full Naval honours at midnight, in a Portsmouth cemetery;

Disappeared by official order, because he was operating unofficially and without permission;

Killed while operating a device to check the presence of an atom bomb on the cruiser;

Guarding the cruiser, and killed by a saboteur.

On May 27, 1956, the *Sunday Times* published a report from its representative in Bonn, reading as follows:

Allegations that the body of Commander Crabb, the frogman, has been recovered from Portsmouth Harbour and details how he is said to have met his death are being circulated in Berlin by Soviet sources who claim to know

more of the circumstances surrounding his last underwater expedition than has been announced.

According to information, reported to come from
Russian naval officers, which cannot be directly
identified, Commander Crabb died as a result of a new
"anti-submarine" device fitted experimentally in the
Soviet cruiser *Ordzhonikidze*.

This is said to be a powerful flap which can be "aimed"
at a frogman and is capable of dragging him under water
to the hull of the vessel and keeping him there . . . until
his oxygen supply is exhausted. He is then "released"
from the magnetic grip and his body is allowed to float
away. . . .

Associated Press reported three days later from
Moscow:

Marshal Zhukov, Soviet Minister of Defence, today
presented a gold, inscribed watch to Rear-Admiral Kotov,
commander of the Soviet Naval Squadron that took
Marshal Bulganin and Mr. Khrushchev to Britain.

In a recent *Pravda* interview Admiral Kotov
denounced the activities of the missing British frogman,
Commander Crabb.

Captain G. F. Stiepanov, commander of the cruiser
Ordzhonikidze, which Crabb was alleged to be inspecting
when he met his death in Portsmouth Harbour, also
received a gold watch.

Western observers here are convinced the presenta-
tions are connected with the apparently successful
thwarting of Crabb's secret mission.

MYSTERY OF THE MISSING FROGMAN
TAKES A NEW TWIST, said the *Daily Express* on
June 16, 1956, when publishing the following story
from Paris:

Strange revelations about Commander Lionel Crabb,

the missing British frogman, were made today by Sir Francis Rose, painter and author.

He said he had a letter from Crabb, written on April 19, the day he disappeared—presumably while diving near the Russian cruiser which brought B and K to Britain.

The letter, postmarked Portsmouth, said: "I'll be in clover the first of the month. I've sold my invention."

Sir Francis, who has lived in Paris a number of years, said he had written to Crabb asking for the return of a £20 loan. Since he received the letter, he continued, these things had happened:

1. After the Crabb story broke, Sir Francis looked through his files to find the letter and hand it over to the authorities, but it had gone.

2. A friend in the British Admiralty appeared in Paris with a cheque which he said represented the debt Crabb owed Sir Francis. The friend expressed the opinion—without substantiation—that Crabb was still alive.

Sir Francis, 46-year-old Scots baronet, suspected that an American friend with whom he was closely associated may know the whereabouts of the missing letter. The American left for home last week.

U.S. security officials have been informed.

A fortnight later the *Daily Telegraph* Bonn correspondent submitted the following story:

Cdr. Crabb, the missing British frogman, is in Moscow's Lefortovo Prison awaiting trial for espionage, according to a report in the West German newspaper *Bild Zeitung* today. It quoted a French Left-wing politician, recently returned from the Soviet capital, as saying that Cdr. Crabb was taken to Moscow after being arrested by Soviet frogmen in Portsmouth Harbour on April 19.

His presence near the three Russian warships which brought Marshal Bulganin and Mr. Khrushchev to

Britain was revealed by secret anti-frogman devices which detected signals from his own equipment. Frogmen from all three Russian ships took part in the chase.

Other statements in the *Bild Zeitung* are: Cdr. Crabb is in solitary confinement; his prison number is 147; at first he refused to give the Russians an account of his work, but "after some days became very open"; he admitted investigating the automatic steering mechanism which enabled the Soviet vessels to avoid shallows and obstacles.

A Russian official, Col. Mjasskoff, offered Cdr. Crabb employment with the Red Fleet and a salary of £1,000 a month. He was assured by Adml. Trobuz, head of the naval counter-espionage service, that he would not be asked to work against Britain, the report added.

Our Paris correspondent telephoned last night: M. Commin, acting secretary general, French Socialist Party and head of the French Socialist delegation to Moscow, formally denied tonight that any member of the delegation had been informed by a Russian that Cdr. Crabb was being held prisoner by the Russians.

A false alarm that Commander Crabb's body might have been found was raised when on August 2, 1956, a skeleton was washed up near Portsmouth—about four miles from where the frogman entered the water during the Russian warships' visit in April. But at the following coroner's inquest the pathologist, Dr. R. Duncan Clay, said that the bones were those of a small man, aged between 35 and 45, and had been in the sea a considerable time—from one to 15 years.

The flow of sensational news about Commander Crabb continued. The next came when the *News Chronicle* published the following message which *Reuter* cabled from Copenhagen on August 7, 1956:

Lionel Crabb, the frogman who went missing when

the Soviet cruiser *Ordzhonikidze* brought B and K to Portsmouth in April, is in Russia, members of the Russian anti-Communist movement, NTS, said today.

The NTS members said they learned from Soviet sailors from the *Ordzhonikidze* and two destroyers which left Copenhagen today after an official visit, that on the cruiser's return voyage from England part of the ship's hospital was strongly blocked off.

There was someone in the area, but none of the crew knew who it was.

Rumours and theories still swept the country, and attempts to solve the Commander Crabb riddle remained in full swing.

On October 7, 1956, Peter Nelson said in the *Empire News*:

We have not, I think, heard the last of the Buster Crabb affair. In diplomatic circles the frogman is again the talking point. . . .

Three months ago the Russian naval officers got medals for undisclosed service on the British trip. Two months ago Commander Lionel Crabb's mother received an Admiralty cheque for £100.

Not so much as a broken flipper has the sea turned up. But there have been reports from Russia that Buster Crabb is not dead, but held prisoner. Should he be alive (and there are plenty who say he is), what will the Russians do? Produce him, like Burgess?

Despite determined and strenuous efforts to find out still more about Commander Crabb, there was a silence of almost seven months. No new information could be dug up, though rumours as to what had happened to the frogman circulated in Naval and civilian circles throughout the United Kingdom, and also in other countries. But it was not until May 5,

1957, that Commander Lionel "Buster" Crabb struck the headlines again. This time it was *Reynolds News* which claimed to have found "the answer to a year-old riddle" when it published the following:

Commander Lionel (Buster) Crabb, the ex-Navy frog-man missing since the B and K visit to Britain a year ago, IS STILL ALIVE.

This was stated categorically last night by a senior Whitehall official.

He said: "We are satisfied that Cdr. Crabb did not die when he went into the water in Portsmouth near the Russian warships, here for the visit of Marshal Bulganin and Mr. Khrushchev.

"We have good reason to believe that he was taken aboard one of the ships and is now being held in Russia."

The official added: "I cannot disclose my proof for saying this, but it would not surprise me if Cdr. Crabb were to be produced at a Moscow press conference one of these days."

In the known facts about the George Medal frogman's disappearance, there is circumstantial evidence in support of the belief that he is still alive.

No body has ever been recovered.

No search was ever carried out which might have led to the recovery of a body.

No Government statement has ever gone further than that the commander "was presumed to have met his death".

Last night I was told that intelligence officers have now discovered that the Russians knew of Commander Crabb's proposed dive before ever he entered the water.

This came through a leakage in the plans of the intelligence group which arranged the operation—they did it without the knowledge or authority of the Government.

So, when he approached the vicinity of the visiting warships, the Russians were fully prepared for him.

It is thought that Russian frogmen seized him and took him aboard the ship by an underwater entrance through an air lock.

Exactly five weeks later it seemed that the time had come when the mystery was on the point of being solved. The *Daily Mail* on June 10, 1957, reported the following important new development:

The body of a man in frogman's clothing was found yesterday in Chichester Harbour.

It was 12 miles from Portsmouth Harbour, where Commander Lionel Crabb vanished in April of last year when Russian warships were anchored there.

The body, headless and handless, was washed up at Pilsey Island, a sandbank at the mouth of Chichester Harbour, near Thorney Aerodrome, R.A.F. officers told Chichester police, who took the body to a mortuary.

The Admiralty has ordered an inquiry. Experts believe the body may be Commander Crabb's. Today Naval authorities at Portsmouth will help in identification.

The man who made the discovery is Mr. John Randall. . . . Last night Mr. Randall, 40-year-old former Merchant Navy man, said: "I was fishing in the harbour when I saw the body."

He told the police that it was encased in a rubber suit that looked like the equipment used by Naval frogmen. Two friends helped him to haul the body into their boat. Then the R.A.F. and the police took over.

Said Mr. Randall last night: "I have been given strict instructions to say no more about this matter."

The fate of "Buster" Crabb, George Medallist and one of the Royal Navy's first frogmen, has never been definitely established. . . .

Next day, June 11, 1957, the *Daily Express* published Mr. Chapman Pincher's article, FROGMAN

CRABB MYSTERY—NOW COMES THIS SEN-
SATIONAL DISCLOSURE, written in Washing-
ton and reading:

COMMANDER LIONEL CRABB was working for
the United States Intelligence Service—not the British—
when he disappeared last year.

American naval authorities denied all knowledge of
Crabb when I questioned them today.

But my inquiries here have revealed that the acute
embarrassment caused by the Crabb incident during the
goodwill visit of Bulganin and Khrushchev to Britain
was due to the following events:

Crabb, a free-lance frogman, approached U.S. Naval
Intelligence agents in London with the proposition
that he would investigate the hull of the cruiser
Ordzhonikidze which had brought the Russian leaders
to Portsmouth.

The agents agreed to pay him according to the value
of the information he could get.

There was the usual understanding that if anything
went wrong the U.S. would disclaim all knowledge of
the operation.

Crabb, who kept in touch with British Intelligence
officers, told some of his contacts.

These men—at the middle level of their departments
—failed to sense the political dangers involved. Instead
of telling their chiefs, who would have stopped Crabb,
they turned a blind eye, hoping they might get some of
the information.

Two of these men were "disciplined" on the orders of
Sir Anthony Eden, then the Prime Minister, when the
Crabb operation came to light. These circumstances put
Sir Anthony Eden into a very difficult position.

He could not reveal the truth without endangering
relations with the U.S. because of agreements between
the two countries on Intelligence.

He could not make a diplomatic denial because the

Russians had revealed that a frogman was seen near the cruiser.

The best he could do was to state truthfully that Crabb's underwater investigation had been completely unauthorised.

Trying to establish a connection between Commander Crabb and the headless and handless body, which was washed up at Chichester, the *Daily Express* said:

Naval frogmen who dived with Crabb on secret experimental work near Portsmouth remembered this:
The Italian two-piece diving suit. . . . "Crabby was cranky about Italian gear," said an old underwater friend. "He shunned 'issue' gear for his Pirelli two-piece." The general issue in Britain is a one-piece.
A TWO-PIECE SUIT WAS FOUND ON THE BODY IN CHICHESTER HARBOUR.
The shirt. . . . "He always wore a faded red-and-white 'pirate' shirt," said his friends.
A COTTON SHIRT WAS FOUND ON THE BODY IN CHICHESTER HARBOUR.
A pathologist, Dr. Donald Plimsoll King, spent 65 minutes examining the frogman's body. He found no clues to the cause of death.
He also found nothing on the frogman's suit to help with identification.
"I examined it most carefully," he said, "but I was unable to trace any Naval serial numbers."
Dr. King last night prepared a 300-word report for the inquest at Chichester today. This is expected to be adjourned for two weeks to allow Naval experts, who will be there, time to collect evidence.
The experts will study Dr. King's findings before the inquest begins.
Last night a Kent C.I.D. sergeant and a policewoman saw 43-year-old Mrs. Margaret Crabb—whose marriage

to the commander was dissolved nearly three years ago—
in the house of a friend in St. Margaret's Bay, Kent. It
is believed they called at the request of the Chichester
police to ask her about possible means of identification.

All other newspapers naturally gave considerable
publicity to the new development in the Commander
Crabb mystery. *The Times,* publishing a report from
its special correspondent of the previous evening
from Chichester, stated:

Experts from the diving school at H.M.S. *Vernon,*
Portsmouth, will attend tomorrow's inquest at Chichester
of the unknown frogman whose headless body was
recovered from the sea near Chichester Harbour yesterday.

The Chichester coroner, Mr. G. F. L. Bridgman, said
last night: "I propose to open the inquest tomorrow
afternoon and adjourn for a fortnight." He said that he
had received the report of Dr. D. King, a pathologist,
who made a *post-mortem* examination, and added:
"Quite honestly, we know little more than we did
before."

It was officially stated at Portsmouth tonight that the
Admiralty had offered to provide expert evidence to help
in identification, if the coroner required it.

Although the identity of the frogman has not been
established yet, Superintendent S. L. Simmonds, of the
Chichester police, states that there must be a strong
assumption that it is Commander Lionel Crabb,
R.N.V.R., who disappeared after trials with underwater
apparatus near Portsmouth on April 19, 1956. The body,
besides being headless, was without hands and quite
obviously had been in the water for some considerable
time. From the action of the currents it could be assumed
that if Commander Crabb was drowned off Portsmouth,
his body would be carried in the direction of Chichester

Harbour, where it was recovered, the superintendent
said. . . .

The *Daily Herald,* after publishing an interview
with Mrs. Margaret Crabb, the ex-Navy commander's
former wife, disclosed:

Police chiefs at Chichester said: "This is not just an
ordinary body—there are security, political and other
reasons for precautions."

The inquest will be opened today—and adjourned.

The coroner, Mr. F. L. Bridgman, indicated yesterday
that the adjournment would be for a fortnight, and
added: "Whether the final inquest will be in public or
in camera, I do not know."

He added: "There is no question at the moment of
having established identification. This is not a straight-
forward case where a person who was with someone at
the time can be called to say, that is the man. We have
appealed to the Admiralty to help us, and they have
agreed to do so. They will be sending experts tomorrow
to see the body and the clothing."

Mr. Bridgman's statement was made after consulta-
tions with Supt. Stanley Simmonds at Chichester police
headquarters.

Frogman Crabb had two hammer-toes.

Dr. D. P. King, consultant pathologist to the Chichester
Hospital Group, has carried out a preliminary post
mortem. The gist of his report is: "Unable to establish
the cause of death. *No easy means of identification
available.*"

Asked about the deformity of the toes, he said: "I feel
a bit doubtful about any deformity. The state of the toes
is not sufficiently abnormal to make any confident statement. There is no gross deformity."

He referred to the upper part of the body held in the
skin-tight rubber frogman suit as "just a collection of
bones," with the hands also missing. But the lower part,

held by a thick rubber band round the waist, he described as "in quite a good state of preservation".

The *Daily Telegraph* published on June 12, 1957,
under the heading "MRS. CRABB UNABLE TO
IDENTIFY FROGMAN—'MR. SMITH' MAY
HOLD CLUE", the following:

Mrs. Margaret Crabb, former wife of Cdr. Lionel
Crabb, the Naval frogman, failed yesterday to identify
the body found off Pilsey Island, Chichester, Sussex, on
Sunday, as that of her ex-husband. . . .

Mrs. Crabb saw the body at Bognor Regis mortuary,
to which it was transferred from Chichester because it
can be preserved better there. She has told the police that
her former husband's feet might be readily identifiable
as he had "buckled" big toes. But lengthy immersion in
the water had distorted the feet.

Earlier an Admiralty expert examined the frogman's
rubber suit at Chichester police station. His report will
be submitted to the police. His preliminary investigation
did not enable him to say whether the suit was of standard
Naval issue. Considerable importance attaches to his
findings.

Although officially unidentified, there can be little
doubt that the body is of Cdr. Crabb. . . .

The clothes on the body could prove a positive means
of identification should the authorities decide to call, if
they can trace him, the man with Cdr. Crabb when he
entered the water. This man, probably the "Matthew
Smith" who signed the register in the Sallyport Hotel,
Portsmouth, when Cdr. Crabb booked in just before
he disappeared, has never been identified publicly.

It is assumed that the man went with the Commander
to the water's edge and he is probably aware of the underclothes the Commander wore. His evidence could be
conclusive.

If the authorities can produce him at the resumed

inquest, they could apply for his identity and evidence to be kept a secret.

Inquiries in Chichester show that some of those in charge of the investigations have received secret briefing on the circumstances relating to Cdr. Crabb's fate. For this reason it is unlikely the full facts about his mission will ever be made public. Cause of death will probably never be known, because of decomposition.

The failure of Mrs. Crabb to make any identification means that, apart from the clothing, the burden will rest on scientific tests and measurements. Unless the clothing is positively identified, or fresh evidence is forthcoming, the body may never be recognised by the authorities as that of Cdr. Crabb.

An inquest on the headless and handless frogman's body, described as an "unidentified man", was opened by Mr. G. F. L. Bridgman, Coroner for Chichester, in the magistrate's court. The only evidence given before the hearing was adjourned until June 26 was that of the coroner's officer, P.C. D. Castleden. Mr. Bridgman put eight questions to the officer:

Mr. Bridgman: This morning did you go to the public mortuary here with me?—Yes, sir.

Did you view the remains of the body of a man?—I did.

And certain articles of clothing?—I did.

Did they consist of a black rubber frogman's suit and flippers?—Yes, sir.

A pair of maroon-coloured bathing trunks?—Yes, sir.

A pair of blue socks?—Yes, sir.

A pair of fawn-coloured combinations?—Yes, sir.

And a pair of blue woollen combinations?—Yes, sir.

The proceedings lasted 45 seconds. Dr. D. P. King, who made the post-mortem examination on the body, was in our court waiting for another inquest.

Mr. Bridgman said last night: "It may be some time before I issue a certificate for the burial of the body. I will not issue a certification while identification remains possible."

The Naval officer who examined the frogman's equipment at Chichester police station yesterday is Lt. W. Y. McLanachan, a torpedo and diving expert from H.M.S. *Vernon,* Portsmouth. He has been placed at the disposal of the West Sussex Constabulary.

The fact that Lt. McLanachan was not at the inquest and that only underclothes, a frogman's suit and flippers were identified, suggests that some secret equipment might have been found on the body.

Also, the mortuary keeper at Chichester was told not to carry out his usual procedure of preparing the body for the post-mortem examination. This would suggest that the police, at the request of Naval authorities, might have removed something.

The same evening, Moscow Radio said in English :

"Nothing about this notorious case could have proved such a sensation as the revelation that the British frogman was carrying out his assignment for the United States Intelligence Service."

Commenting on the events 14 months ago, the radio said :

"It was suddenly learned that an English diver had secretly tried to examine the underwater part of the Soviet cruiser for espionage purposes."

Next morning *The Times* quoted Lieutenant W. Y. McLanachan as having said that the equipment was "definitely not Admiralty type", and went on :

. . . he said at his home at Fratton, near Portsmouth, that it was the sort of suit that could be bought anywhere.

Lieutenant McLanachan, aged 43, said he first met Commander Lionel Crabb in 1948, at H.M.S. *Vernon,* where Commander Crabb was undergoing a refresher course. He declined to comment on how far his report would help to identify the remains. All he saw was the equipment.

The same morning the *Daily Sketch* published the following sensations:

The headless frogman found in Chichester Harbour WAS 48-year-old "Buster" Crabb.

A Naval officer has identified clothing inside the frogman's suit.

He is Lieut. William McLanachan, a member of Crabb's wartime unit.

McLanachan said last night: "This has been a sad day for me.

"Commander Crabb was a brave man."

Lieut. McLanachan spoke after cycling home . . . from the diving school, H.M.S. *Vernon*.

He went on: "I met him in 1948 at H.M.S. *Vernon* when he was on a refresher course. I have known him since. I know the type of clothing he would wear."

He examined the torn frogman suit, two pairs of woollen combinations and a maroon bathing suit found on the body.

The frogman's suit is of Italian pattern. "It's the sort that could be bought in any sports outfitter," he said.

The inquest will be resumed on June 26.

The riddle deepened, however, when it was disclosed that, three days before the headless and handless body in a frogman's suit was washed up at Pilsey Island, three Russian submarines had passed through the English Channel. Virtually everybody was highly interested in what was the real truth about Commander Crabb. Consequently, not only in Portsmouth and throughout the United Kingdom, but also abroad, new rumours swept the countries, and much that had been said before came up again. Two main theories, however, were most widespread and considered by many to be the solution of the mystery.

The first one was:

That when attempting to examine the cruiser *Ordzhonikidze,* Commander Crabb was captured by the Russians, taken to Russia and interrogated. When he refused to tell the Russians any secrets, they killed him, and the three Russian submarines which passed the English coast three days before his body was washed up near Chichester Harbour disposed of the body so that it could be found and identified in England.

The second theory expressed the following idea:

That the headless and handless body is not that of Commander Crabb. For one reason or another, the Russian submarines which passed three days before the body was washed up near Chichester Harbour planted a "man who never was" on the British authorities, in order to put an end, once and for all, to the mystery. The real Commander Crabb may be alive in Russia.

On June 16, 1957, *Reynolds News* published the following:

BRITISH security experts believe the riddle of the headless frogman—assumed to be the remains of Cdr. Lionel "Buster" Crabb—may never be solved.

They say that the one fact which may emerge is that the body washed up a week ago in Chichester Harbour is NOT that of Cdr. Crabb, missing 14 months ago during the visit of the Soviet leaders B and K.

The Commander is alive and in Russian hands, British security agents still believe. They base their belief on reports from behind the Iron Curtain since his disappearance.

Commander Crabb, 46, dived into Portsmouth Harbour to make an underwater survey of the crack Russian cruiser *Ordzhonikidze*.

His action, for an intelligence group working without Government authority, was to discover the secret of the cruiser's speed, which is considerably more than that of similar British ships.

The last man to have contact with the Commander before he vanished was an intelligence officer who stayed at the same hotel in the name of "Matthew Smith".

It has been stated that he could say if the body washed up was that of Commander Crabb—the frogman's ex-wife Margaret has been unable to identify it—because he was the one person who knew what clothing was worn for the dive.

BUT I CAN REVEAL THAT HE DOES NOT KNOW WHAT BUSTER CRABB WORE UNDER HIS FROGMAN KIT.

The two men parted three hours before the dive. The Commander went alone to his hotel bedroom to put on the clothing he wore under his diving suit.

Q.: If the headless frogman was not Cdr. Crabb, who was he?

A.: A British security agent said last night: One theory is that the body has been planted.

Q.: Is it feasible that someone would think of planting a body?

A.: British Intelligence did this during the war, as described in the story of "The Man Who Never Was".

Q.: How could such an action have been prepared?

A.: Three Russian submarines were reported in the Channel three days before the body was washed up.

Q.: Why should such a macabre deception be attempted?

A.: It would bring the Crabb story dramatically back into the news and so, when the Commander was revealed to be alive, the propaganda effect would be all the greater.

If the plant theory were correct, the attempt failed because the headless body does not match Commander Crabb's physique in one detail.

He was hammer-toed. Even allowing for the mummifying process undergone by the body, the bone of the second toe on each foot would show signs of having been overlapped by the big toe.

No such sign has been found.

Footnote: Devon police yesterday ruled out the possibility that the body is that of 22-year-old Eric Wilton, of Richmond, Surrey, a frogman drowned off Dartmouth in 1955.

The official investigations into the Commander Crabb mystery came to an end when the inquest was resumed on June 26, 1957, at Chichester. The *Daily Telegraph* published on June 27 the following report:

The body of a frogman found floating in the sea near Chichester Harbour was that of Cdr. Lionel Kenneth Philip Crabb, who disappeared near Portsmouth a year ago, said the Chichester Coroner, Mr. G. F. L. BRIDGMAN, at the inquest yesterday. A chain of coincidences had convinced him of this.

Recording an open verdict, the coroner said it was impossible to determine the cause of death. "We have all been warned from time to time in the legal profession about a chain being as strong as its weakest link, but there is also such a thing as a number of incidents which are minor indications building up to a conclusion, which I do not think can be resisted.

"I think it would be beyond all our ideas of possible

coincidence if all these different things, the size of the feet, the scar, the colour of hair, the sort of legs, the supply of identical suit, if all these things were to be put down to sheer coincidence.

"Looking at the evidence in this case I am quite satisfied that the remains which were found in Chichester Harbour on June 9 were those of Cdr. Crabb, who was last seen, by a witness called today, on April 17, 1956, in London."

The remains were in such a condition that it was impossible to obtain any evidence of the cause of death. From rust-marks found on the legs of the frogman's suit it would seem that the body was caught up by the feet and legs.

The lower part was caught up in some position which protected it from "the process, both mechanical and animal," of the sea, with the result that the body was practically destroyed down to the waist, but remained in good preservation below that point.

The inquest lasted less than an hour. Mr. A. W. GEDDES represented Mrs. Beatrice Crabb, the Commander's mother and next of kin. Mr. B. M. STEPHENSON, Treasury Solicitor, appeared for the Crown. Neither questioned any of the 10 witnesses.

When the inquest, which had been adjourned since June 11, reopened, Dr. Donald King, pathologist, who examined the headless frogman, told the coroner that the dead man's feet measured $8\frac{3}{4}$ in., small feet for a man, and had distorted big toes. There were signs of a scar on the left knee.

He formed the opinion that the body was that of a small man about 5 ft. 6 in. in height. His legs were muscular and straight, and apart from the toes there were no other deformation. He estimated the body had been in the sea at least six months and could well have been for 14 months.

Evidence of finding the body in the sea was given by JOHN RANDALL, of Bosham, Hants. He said he was out fishing with two other men when he saw an object floating in the water. On reaching it he realised it was the body of a man in a frogman's suit.

Details of Cdr. Crabb's service career were given by Mr. GORDON WILLIAM BOSTOCK, temporary clerical officer in the Admiralty Reserves Department, the only Naval witness.

In 1952 Crabb was promoted to the rank of commander and in April, 1955, was finally released from Naval service. Since that date he had not been employed at all in the services of the Navy, nor done any training.

Details of his service life during the war with Cdr. Crabb were given by SIDNEY JAMES KNOWLES, of Geoffrey Street, Preston, supervisor of a swimming pool.

He said that in December, 1939, he joined the Navy and two years later met Crabb and did underwater work with him. Elaborating how Crabb got a scar on his left knee, Knowles said that in 1945 they were in Leghorn, Italy, together.

At that time captains of ships were instructed to hang rolls of barbed wire below the watermarks of their ships to protect them against Italian frogmen. One morning he and Crabb dived to find limpet mines beneath an American ship.

"We had to swim under it. While we were going down a tug passing overhead cast a wash, throwing both of us against the barbed wire. When we got back I noticed Cdr. Crabb had a wound on his left knee and I dressed it.

"Three weeks later, when I was working with him again, I noticed a scar in the shape of an inverted Y about the size of a shilling piece on the left side of his left knee."

After the war he saw Crabb from time to time. Crabb then had worn a two-piece rubber suit which differed from others because it had a neck seal instead of a hood.

Miss AMY THOMAS, of Hans Road, Chelsea, manageress of service flatlets, said Crabb occupied one for five years until April, 1956. Early that month he said he was going away for a few days and eventually left on April 17. He never returned.

He had been engaged on some business while he was living there. She thought he had been working in the furniture trade.

Crabb's former wife, Mrs. MARGARET ELAINE CRABB, 42, said she formerly lived in St. Margaret's Bay and had been a typist. She and Crabb were married on March 15, 1952, and they lived together until April, 1953, when she began proceedings for divorce.

She obtained a decree by an undefended petition which was made absolute in December, 1954. During her married life Crabb was serving as a commander in the R.N.V.R.

Mrs. Crabb bore out details of her former husband's height and other points given by the doctor. She agreed he was short, had muscular straight legs and had what she described as "hammer-toes".

She thought he took a size six in shoes. When she went to identify the body she could not say from looking at the feet whether it was her former husband, but equally she could not say he was not.

Frogman's suits he issued to Cdr. Crabb were described by ERIC BLAKE, of Leatherhead, managing director of Heinke & Co., of Bermondsey, manufacturers of underwater swimsuits. He said he had supplied Crabb with three suits, the last one in October, 1955.

It was unusual, as it had a neck seal without a hood. He had been shown the outfit recovered from the sea and found it identical with the type he had sold to Cdr. Crabb.

After the inquest, Mr. A. W. Geddes, solicitor for Cdr. Crabb's mother, Mrs. Beatrice Crabb, issued a statement in which he said:

"There have been many irresponsible conjectures regarding the last operation upon which Cdr. Crabb was engaged prior to his disappearance, including even suggestions that he was in the employ of a foreign power.

"It is desired therefore to emphasise that every particle of evidence in our possession points conclusively to the fact that this very gallant gentleman died, as he had lived, in the service of our own country and of no other."

Asked if he could elaborate on this, Mr. Geddes replied: "I cannot say any more. Our hands are tied."

An Admiralty spokesman said last night: "The Admiralty can add nothing to its original statement or to the statement of the Prime Minister."

No evidence was given by anyone at the inquest about the last two days of Crabb's life, April 18 and 19, 1956. The man who signed the register at a Portsmouth hotel as "Matthew Smith", who was said to be with Crabb and who paid the bill after Crabb vanished, did not give evidence.

The same morning the *Daily Express* published the following article by Chapman Pincher and Arnold Latchman:

A CORONER DECIDED YESTERDAY THAT THE FROGMAN FOUND IN CHICHESTER HARBOUR A FORTNIGHT AGO WAS COMMANDER LIONEL CRABB. BUT THAT DOES NOT END THE RIDDLE. IT LEAVES IT IN A MAZE OF CONFLICTING STATEMENTS: —

THE CRABB FAMILY solicitor, Mr. Alastair Geddes, said immediately after the inquest: —

"There have been many irresponsible conjectures regarding the last operation upon which Commander Crabb was engaged, including even the suggestion that he was in the employ of a foreign power.

"It is desired therefore to emphasise that every particle of evidence in our possession points conclusively to the fact that this very gallant gentleman died as he had lived in the service of our country and of no other."

QUESTION: Which "foreign power"?

ANSWER: The suggestion was that Crabb was working for the Americans.

ADMIRALTY OFFICIALS, at the time Crabb disappeared and again last night, said that he "did not return from a test dive which took place in connection with trials of certain underwater apparatus" in Stokes Bay, three miles from Portsmouth Harbour.

QUESTION: But not in Portsmouth itself?

ANSWER: From Moscow—

THE RUSSIANS announced that they spotted a frogman operating near Soviet warships in Portsmouth Harbour during the visit of Bulganin and Khrushchev.

QUESTION: Then Crabb *was* working for the Navy in the harbour?

ANSWER: A year ago—

THE PRIME MINISTER, then Sir Anthony Eden, told M.P.s: "It would not be in the public interest to disclose the circumstances in which Commander Crabb met his death . . . what was done was done without the authority or knowledge of Ministers."

QUESTION: So Crabb was disowned?

ANSWER: That was confirmed at the inquest yesterday.

THE ADMIRALTY representative, Mr. George Bostock, told the coroner: "Since April 8, 1955, when he was released from Naval service, Commander Crabb has not been in the service of the Navy at all."

NOW COMES A THEORY THAT WOULD SEEM WILDLY FAR-FETCHED IF IT HAD NOT BEEN FOR THE CASE OF "THE MAN WHO NEVER WAS" DURING THE WAR.

THERE is a strong suspicion among some officials that Crabb's body has not been in the water for 14 months.

Extraordinary coincidence: It reappeared only a few days after Russian submarines passed through the English Channel on the way to Egypt.

These officials suspect Crabb may have been captured by the Russians in Portsmouth Harbour and taken to Leningrad for prolonged interrogation.

The Russians, in this theory, finally killed him and "planted" the body to deceive British Intelligence.

Why should the Russians attempt such a deception? Last night a former Intelligence officer explained it this way:

Crabb knew many of the secrets of British underwater intelligence.

Though he was not the type of man who would willingly divulge such secrets, Intelligence authorities in London are satisfied that the Russians would stop at nothing to secure them.

Having interrogated Crabb for months, the Russians would not want the British to know.

Hence the possibility that the body was deposited to give the impression that it had been 14 months in the water.

At yesterday's inquest it was indicated that the body might have been immersed only six months.

And rust marks were found on the legs of the frogman's suit as if the body had been caught up in a metal object. . . .

On July 4, 1957, the Crabb affair was again raised in Parliament when Mr. Rankin (Glasgow, Govan, Labour) asked the Prime Minister if he could now make a statement on the circumstances in which Commander Crabb disappeared in Portsmouth Harbour.

Mr. Macmillan replied: "I have no statement to make on this subject."

Mr. Rankin then asked: "Is the Prime Minister aware that after the inquest the solicitor representing the Crabb family stated that Commander Crabb had

died in the service of his country? Does the Prime
Minister accept that view; and if he does, will he see
that the appropriate pension is issued to the widow
in addition to the solitary *ex gratia* payment of £10
which so far had been made?"

Mr. Macmillan said he would look into the second
part of the question. As for the first part, he could
make no further statement. He must stand by the
statement made by Sir Anthony Eden in the debate
on May 14 last year.

On July 5, 1957, the body of the frogman was at
last buried. The *Daily Telegraph* made the following
short announcement next day:

Cdr. Lionel Crabb, 46, the frogman whose body was
found off Chichester on June 9, after he disappeared at
Portsmouth in April last year during a visit by Russian
warships, was buried at Portsmouth yesterday. There
were no official representatives of the Navy at the funeral.

Officially the last chapter of the Commander Crabb
affair had thus been written.

II

What Is The Truth?

This question puzzled not only Commander
Crabb's relatives and close friends, but also newspapermen and others interested in the mystery. It
was commonly felt that the inquest had not thrown
full light on whether the headless and handless body

was really that of Commander Crabb, and more and
more people began to express the opinion that the
coroner's findings were the outcome of stringent
instructions which he had received from the "highest
quarters".

The main questions which puzzled the public
were:

How was it that neither the pathologist nor Commander Crabb's ex-wife were able to find any
deformation of the toes when first examining the
body, and what made the pathologist at the resumed
inquest admit deformation of the toes?

How was it that, after a careful examination of the
body, the pathologist did not find a scar on the body's
left knee, and what made him admit, at the resumed
inquest, the presence of a scar?

Did the pathologist disclose his real findings on
the examination of the body before he received orders
to confirm such findings as were required for a
declaration that the body was that of Commander
Crabb?

Why was Lieutenant McLanachan, who had
examined the equipment, not called upon to give
conclusive evidence at the inquest, and why was
"Mr. Matthew Smith" not called?

Did it not occur to either the pathologist or the
coroner that it was more than strange that the head
and BOTH hands were missing from the body—all
the vital parts which could have provided conclusive
identification? Why was this not fully gone into at
the inquest, especially as it was known that Russian
submarines passed the British coast three days prior

to the appearance of the body, and that Commander Crabb mysteriously vanished while diving in the vicinity of the Russian cruiser *Ordzhonikidze?*

The more the Commander Crabb mystery was discussed, the more those interested in the riddle came to the conclusion that the inquest had not solved the mystery. Wilder than ever rumours continued to circulate.

In Portsmouth the following belief was—and perhaps still is—quite common: "Crabbie's" body was not found—the body which was buried as Commander Lionel Kenneth Philip Crabb, O.B.E., G.M., R.N.V.R., was a Russian plant, aimed at convincing the British authorities and the British public that the frogman was dead and so put an end to this object of widespread public interest. "Crabbie is in Russia and alive," many in Portsmouth still believed.

In London the following theory was—and perhaps still is—quite common: Commander Crabb is not dead—he is probably imprisoned in Russia. The body which was washed up near Chichester may have been in Crabb's frogman suit, but unfortunately this possibility was not gone into at the resumed inquest. But for this occurrence one can't really blame the coroner or the witnesses, as it is obvious that they all acted on instructions from some higher authority. "To Crabbie", some of his friends still drank when speaking of the vanished hero. They do not—and do not want—to believe that he is dead.

In other parts of the country other theories were

discussed. They all expressed the firm belief that the headless and handless body which at the inquest at Chichester was declared as that of Commander Crabb was not really the commander. Many called the buried body "The Man Who Never Was" and refused to believe that during the alleged 14 months in the sea the body would have lost its head and BOTH hands. "Had the head, a hand and an arm, or part of the arms, been missing, it would have looked possible. But the fact that both hands were missing strengthens the theory that this was not the work of the sea but of someone who had a special interest in preventing a conclusive identification of the body," is the sincere opinion expressed privately by a pathologist, who had no connection with the Crabb affair whatsoever.

The Crabb mystery was still alive with individual members of the public. Newspapermen and others still went out of their way untiringly to pick up any scrap of new evidence about Commander Crabb, hoping that they might perhaps still be able to solve the mystery. But despite great efforts, only very few new facts came to light.

On October 2, 1957, Commander Crabb was, however, in the news again, when the *Daily Express* published the following:

The killing of Frogman Crabb is now being claimed by speakers of Communist Party rallies in Russia as a perfect example of Communist "vigilance".

Commander Crabb, say the speakers, was observed by the ship's watch, then killed by starting the ship's propeller at the right moment.

Almost six months later, on March 25, 1958, the
Liverpool Daily Post announced in bold letters:

KHRUSHCHEV ADMITS IT: WE KILLED CRABB.

WHAT *DID* HAPPEN THAT NIGHT TWO YEARS AGO IN THE WATERS ROUND THE ORDZHONIKIDZE?

NEW light has been shed on the mysterious fate of
Commander Lionel Crabb by no less an authority than
Mr. Khrushchev. In a secret report on his visit to Britain
in 1956 with the Soviet Prime Minister, Marshal
Bulganin, the contents of which have just been divulged,
he makes direct reference to Crabb.

The frogman disappeared on April 19, 1956, in
Portsmouth Harbour while testing underwater apparatus.
Nearby was the Russian cruiser *Ordzhonikidze* which
had brought the Russian leaders to Britain the day
before.

Russia complained later that a frogman had been spying on the warship, and although Britain expressed regret
for the incident, both she and America denied that Crabb
was operating on their behalf.

Over a year later Crabb's body was found floating in
Chichester Harbour. But the riddle of how he died was
never solved. The body offered no clue.

Now Mr. Khrushchev, it seems, has given the answer.
He says that an English frogman spying on the Soviet
warship had been "rendered harmless".

In May, 1956, two senior Russian naval officers
received awards "for distinguishing themselves while in
Britain. . . ."

This report again stirred up considerable public
interest in the Commander Crabb mystery, and new
speculations as to what actually happened were on
almost everybody's lips. The same was the case when

renewed reports from Scandinavia, France, the Middle East and other countries reached Britain, divulging that Red sailors who had been in Portsmouth during the B and K visit, on various occasions confirmed that on April 19, 1956, a British frogman had been captured by Soviet swimmers, that he had been imprisoned in the cruiser's hospital and taken out of Britain. Due to the fact that each of these reports emphasised that this information was given on different occasions by various individuals—each such disclosure and informer unconnected with the other—the belief continues to be that the headless and handless body in Commander Crabb's frogman suit was definitely not that of the Naval hero, but that the whole affair was a sinister Russian plant.

Though the interest in the Crabb mystery did not wane and though continuous attempts were made to solve the riddle, no further headway was made.

Then, in November, 1959, full light was at last thrown upon the mystery which had caused such great public interest in Britain and most of the other countries of the civilised world. This revelation came in the form of the Russian Secret *Dossier* on the captured frogman, which was smuggled out from behind the Iron Curtain by secret agents, and which reached Britain in November, 1959.

The Russian Secret *Dossier*, "THE COMMANDER CRABB CASE" contains the original reports from Captain Stiepanov, commander of the cruiser *Ordzhonikidze*, from State Security officers who escorted Commander Crabb to Moscow, from Investigation Judges, Prison Commandant and prison officers, interrogators, and all those who had direct dealings with the British Naval commander.

At the conference of all the heads of State Security Forces of all the Iron Curtain countries, held in Moscow from August 3-10, 1959, it was ruled that the Secret Police Headquarters of all the countries of the "People's Democracies" should receive "translations of secret Soviet *dossiers* which could help the foreign comrades of the State Security Headquarters to learn from the experiences of our best-trained Investigation Judges how to go about in seemingly hopeless cases and what methods and tactics to apply to break down the prisoner without the application of drugs, violence, or other such methods".

One of these *dossiers*, which were considered to be "useful examples of how to go about in even the trickiest situation", was the Secret *Dossier* of Commander Crabb. Together with other secret *dossiers* it was officially translated into Bulgarian, Czech, Hungarian, German, Polish and Rumanian, and in due course sent out to the Russian Chief Instructors in these Iron Curtain countries, who are the big bosses behind the scenes, and who in fact direct not only the Soviet puppet governments and Communist parties, but also the individual State Security Forces.

How the Russian Secret *Dossier* about Commander Crabb was obtained and how ways and means were found to smuggle it out from behind the Iron Curtain can naturally not be revealed, as this would endanger those men and women who, in the Soviet rear, daily risk their lives to obtain valuable information for the Western world. But it can be revealed that the material from these secret sources has been most thoroughly checked and it has been established and confirmed that the documents made available by them, are absolutely genuine.

The *dossier* of "The Commander Crabb Case"— though written in the matter-of-fact style of officers' reports—makes most interesting and even thrilling reading. But, what is more, it clearly reveals the extraordinary methods and tactics which the Russians use and, besides solving the Commander Crabb mystery, is thus also a most valuable document of Soviet interrogation, prison and other practices.

In order to acquaint the reader with the actual secret document, nothing has been changed or added, and the complete *dossier* is therefore reproduced on the following pages in its true translation.

III

Russia Gives the Answer

REPORT FROM CAPTAIN G. F. STIEPANOV

Wednesday, April 18, 1956. 21.10 hours.

Portsmouth shore agent O2SD submitted the following:

Information reveals that U.S. Naval Intelligence intends to carry out extensive examinations of our warships, anchored in Stokes Bay. According to this information British Naval Authorities know of these plans and, having been promised a share in any data

Photograph of title page of the Secret *Dossier*, disclosing that the translation from Russian was made in Moscow in order to help the Iron Curtain Security bosses to learn from the experience of Soviet Interrogators.

The text makes very awkward reading, probably due to the translator having decided to concentrate more on the accuracy of the translation than on fluent reading.

It is interesting to note that there is a typing error in the document.

BERICHT VON KAPITÄN G.F.STJEPANOFF.

Mittwoch,den 18.April 1956. 21,10 Uhr.

Portsmouth Uferagent O2SD meldete folgendes:

Erhaltene Nachrichten enthüllen,daß der Marine Nachrichten=
dienst der Vereinigten Staaten vorhat weitgehende Unterwas=
seruntersuchungen unserer Kriegsschiffe,die in Stokes Bay
ankern,durchzuführen. Gemäß dieser Nachrichten sind die
britischen Marinebehörden über diese Pläne unterrichtet und
haben offensichtlich keine Vorsichtsmaßregeln unternommen,
um jedwelche Untersuchungen ihrer mächtigen Verbündeten zu
verbieten,da ihnen anheimgestellt wurde,daß sie an jedwel=
chen Ermittlungen Anteil haben werden.

Portsmouth Uferagent O2SD hat festgestellt,daß der bekannte
britische Taucher Kommandant Lionel Krabb,berühmt als Buster
Krabb,gestern mit nur leichtem Gepäck von London eintraf,ein
Zimmer im Sallyport Hotel,das unweit des Portsmouth Hafens
steht,mietete,und daß sich ihm später ein Freund,der ein
klares Marineurbild ist,und der sich in das Hotelregister im
Namen Smit eintrug,anschloß. Er hatte ebenfalls nur leichtes
Gepäck und kam von London. Seine Aussprache ist britisch und
nicht amerikanisch,was darauf hinweisen mag,daß er ein bri=
tischer Nachrichtenoffizier ist,der wahrscheinlich beauf=
tragt ist die Gesamthandlung zu überwachen,und Krabb zu ver=
nehmen,wenn er von seiner Aufklärung zurückkommt.

Krabb und Smit werden ununterbrochen von unseren Landagenten
überwacht,sodaß,falls Krabb und Smit irgendwelche verdächti=
gen Züge machen,sofort eine chiffrierte Meldung vom Land aus
an unseren Funktelegraphisten gefunkt werden kann.

Habe sofortige 24=stündige Wache angeordnet und habe die
Nachricht an die Kommandanten eines jeden Schiffes unseres
Marinegeschwaders weitergeleitet.

Habe die chiffrierte Abfassung dieses Berichts um 22,18 Uhr,
18.4.1956 ans Hauptquartier gefunkt. Empfing um 23,51 Uhr,
18.4.1956 Empfangsbestätigung,besagend:

„KOMORD 22/18 UHR 18/4/1956 EMPFANGEN = MOSKOM"

Gez.: Kapitän G.F.Stjepanoff.

Bericht gelesen: Konteradmiral V.F.Kotoff

Photograph of page from the Secret *Dossier*. Report from Capt. G. F. Styepanov.

It will be noted that both the Russian names are spelled in the Continental fashion and that Commander Crabb's name is spelled with a "K" instead of "C". This is obviously due to the fact that the Russians spell his name with a "K" and the official translator in Moscow was apparently not familiar with the right spelling. The name Smith is persistently spelled without an "h", which may be for the reason that there is no "h" in the Russian alphabet. The style of this report is very clumsy, and it would appear that the translator did his utmost to make an exact translation of the Russian original, even at the expense of producing less fluent reading.

obtained, have obviously not taken any precautions to prohibit any investigations made by their mighty Ally.

Portsmouth shore agent O2SD has established that the well-known British Naval frogman, Commander Lionel Crabb, famous as Buster Crabb, arrived yesterday from London with only light luggage, and has taken a room at the Sallyport Hotel, near Portsmouth Harbour, where he was later joined by a friend, an obvious Naval type, who has signed the hotel register in the name of Smith. He too has only light luggage and has come from London. His accent is British, not American, which would make it appear that he is a British Naval Intelligence Officer, probably instructed to supervise the whole action, and to question Crabb when he returns from his reconnaissance.

Both Crabb and Smith are under round-the-clock observation by our shore agents so that a coded message can at once be radioed from shore to our radio-telegraphist, should Crabb and Smith make any suspicious moves.

Have ordered an immediate 24-hour watch and have transmitted the information to the commanders of each vessel of our Naval squadron.

Coded version of this report radioed to headquarters at 22.18 hours, 18.4.1956. Acknowledgement received at 23.51 hours, 18.4.1956, reading:

"KOMORD 22/18 HOURS 18/4/1956 RECEIVED— MOSKOM"

Signed: Capt. G. F. Stiepanov.

Report read: Rear-Admiral V. F. Kotov.

REPORT FROM CAPTAIN G. F. STIEPANOV

Thursday, April 19, 1956. 18.00 hours.

At 07.31 hours, Radio Officer Lieutenant K. M. Antonov received a coded message from shore agent O2SD which he immediately handed over to me. The message read:

> "0700 HOURS CRABB LEFT SALLYPORT HOTEL CARRYING FROGMAN OUTFIT STOP UNDERSTOOD CARRYING OUT UNDERWATER EXAMINATIONS ORDZHONIKIDZE FOR UNITED STATES INTELLIGENCE STOP ACCOMPANIED BY OTHER MAN BELIEVED TO BE HIGH RANKING NAVAL OFFICIAL —O2SD"

On decoding message, ordered renewed re-checking of all the alarm devices and a still more intensified watch. Also informed Rear-Admiral V. F. Kotov of shore agent's message, and received his instructions, also given to all the other vessels of our Naval Squadron:

"Keep intensive watch for the frogman. Should he be discovered, everything possible must be done to get him on board ship alive."

At 07.43 hours ordered Radio Officer Lieutenant Antonov to send out to headquarters the coded message which shore agent O2SD transmitted at 07.31 hours.

Despite the most careful watch on all the vessels of our Naval Squadron no trace of the frogman could be spotted. Not only I, but also Rear-Admiral Kotov, with whom I was in constant touch, began to consider that some unexpected circumstances had forced the British frogman to abandon his plans.

In order to obtain further information on the matter, I instructed Radio Officer Lieutant Antonov to contact shore agent O2SD. But his call-sign remained unanswered. So we abandoned our attempts in order not to alert the British counter espionage.

To keep headquarters informed of the full developments, I ordered Radio Officer Lieutenant Antonov at 08.15 hours to radio the following coded message:

"NO TRACE FOUND STOP PLANS SEEM CALLED OFF STOP CONTINUE KEEPING MOST INTENSIFIED WATCH—KOMORD"

At 08.24 hours the *Ordzhonikidze* alarm devices sounded a warning.

This was the pre-arranged signal for four of our best swimmers to dive into the muddy water, they having been given orders to capture the British frogman alive if anyway possible. Rear-Admiral Kotov was at once notified of what was going on so that he could instruct the Commanders of the other vessels to help our swimmers if need be.

The British frogman managed to elude our swimmers and succeeded in proceeding near to the destroyer *Smotriashchin*. There reinforcements from the destroyer dived into the water and cut off the escape route. Without a struggle the fugitive was captured and escorted back to the *Ordzhonikidze*. When the position was clear, at 08.39 hours I ordered Radio Officer Lieutenant Antonov to radio the following coded message to headquarters:

"FROGMAN INTERCEPTED—KOMORD"

While the British frogman was being taken through the air-lock door on board the *Ordzhonikidze*, the following coded message was received from headquarters at 08.54 hours by Radio Officer Lieutenant Antonov:

"DETAIN INTERROGATE STOP SUBMIT REPORT ON INFORMATION OBTAINED—MOSKOM"

Saw prisoner on B-deck at 09.05 hours together with Political Officer K. G. Vosensky, and asked him in Russian:

"Who are you?"

When the captured frogman did not reply, I repeated my question in English. Even then the prisoner remained silent. I decided not to continue the interrogation on the spot because some officers and men were around and were obviously interested in what was going on. So I had the frogman escorted to hospital quarters, as I considered this the most suitable place on the cruiser, because, if by any chance the British had noticed what had been going on and decided to make inquiries, I could declare quite plausibly that the prisoner was one of our sailors who had fallen ill.

With the hospital cabin closely guarded, together with Political Officer Vosensky, and the Intelligence Officers A. A. Shcherkin and V. B. Dmitriev, I continued interrogating the captured frogman at 09.10 hours in English as follows:

"Who are you?"

No answer.

"We know that you are the British Naval frogman,

Commander Lionel Crabb. Do you admit this?"
No answer.

I told the prisoner that his foolish attitude of
stubborn silence would not help him, made it clear
that we had information about his underwater
examination of the *Ordzhonikidze's* hull, that we
knew he was working for American Naval Intelligence, and that his friend who posed as "Smith" at
the Sallyport Hotel was a Senior Naval Officer. I
also told him that his answering my question would
help him, whereas if he continued to keep silent it
would go strongly against him. But he still refused
to speak.

Political Officer Vosensky then took over, but was
also unable to make any headway. The same applied
to attempts made by Intelligence Officers Shcherkin
and Dmitriev. When it was obvious that Crabb was
not going to change his attitude, we abandoned any
further attempts at 10.25 hours. At 11.25 hours the
following coded report was radioed to headquarters:

"INTERROGATION FAILED DUE TO PERSISTENT
SILENCE OF PRISONER TO EVERY QUESTION STOP
ADVISE WHETHER APPLICATION OF STRONGER
MEASURES REQUIRED STOP HE IS COMMANDER
LIONEL CRABB ALSO KNOWN AS BUSTER CRABB
46 YEAR OLD WELL KNOWN BRITISH NAVAL FROG-
MAN HOLDER OF GEORGE MEDAL STOP HIS MISSION
WAS EXAMINATION ORDZHONIKIDZE HULL FOR
UNITED STATES AND PRESUMABLY BRITISH NAVAL
INTELLIGENCE STOP ALARM DEVICES SHOWED
MEASURING APPARATUS THESE WERE FOUND ON

HIM STOP AWAITING FURTHER ORDERS—
KOMORD"

At 12.05 hours received the following coded headquarter message reply:

"NO FURTHER MEASURES ABANDON INTERROGATION STOP KEEP K DRUGGED IN HOSPITAL BED STOP IN CASE OF UNEXPECTED DEVELOPMENTS BANDAGE FACE DECLARE AS SICK MEMBER OF CREW STOP NO FURTHER COMMUNICATION ON SUBJECT UNLESS FURTHER DEVELOPMENTS—MOSKOM"

After decoding message, gave orders to strip prisoner and to put him into hospital bed. All articles found on frogman were put together in a Red Cross box and stowed away safely. Ordered Medical Officer N. I. Yeremenko to inject prisoner and then to bandage his face for any event. But when M.O. attempted to inject prisoner, he suddenly put up a fierce fight and knocked the M.O. down. Was then overpowered by guards and injected. At 13.15 hours M.O. reported that prisoner was heavily asleep.

Prisoner is continuously guarded by two Security Officers who are on five-hour watches, and M.O. repeats injections before prisoner regains consciousness.

Coded version of this report radioed to headquarters at 22.26 hours 19.4.1956.

Acknowledgement received at 00.40 hours 20.4.1956, reading:

"KOMORD 2226 HOURS 19/4/1956 RECEIVED—
MOSKOM"

Signed: Capt. G. F. Stiepanov.
Report read: Rear-Admiral V. F. Kotov.

REPORT FROM CAPTAIN G. F. STIEPANOV
Friday, April 20, 1956. 21.00 hours.

Portsmouth shore agent O2SD submitted the following:

Commander Crabb's friend who poses as "Smith" yesterday waited until early afternoon at the waterfront. Twice he went to the nearby telephone booth and each time returned to his previous place, after a few minutes. At 14.15 hours he again went to the telephone booth and, after a two-minute conversation, walked towards the town. Trailed him but lost him because I did not have the necessary facilities when he was picked up by a black Rover saloon. Number-plate was not clearly visible from my place, but car appeared to be an official Navy or police car. Later "Smith" returned to Sallyport Hotel, collected the light luggage, paid the bill for Commander Crabb and himself, and afterwards left by rail for London.

All attempts to find out more about the frogman's direct mission have up till now failed, though a number of well-versed agents did their utmost to find concrete information. It appears that the Crabb affair is considered top-secret by the Naval Authorities. We, however, continue our investigation, and it is possible that valuable information may come to light.

Portsmouth shore agent O2SD informed me that he will submit his next report tomorrow at 20.00 hours and we agreed meanwhile not to communicate by radio with one another, to prevent British Intelligence being alerted.

Medical Officer N. I. Yeremenko's report states

that the prisoner is kept drugged round-the-clock. His face and hands are kept bandaged in case of sudden unforeseen British moves. While sleeping, he is being artificially fed. Though unconscious, he is being closely guarded by night and day.

Coded version of this report radioed to headquarters at 22.10 hours 20.4.1956.

Acknowledgement received at 23.54 hours, 20.4.1956, reading:

"KOMORD 2210 HOURS 20/4/1956 RECEIVED—MOSKOM"

Signed: Capt. G. F. Stiepanov.

Report read: Rear-Admiral V. F. Kotov.

REPORT FROM CAPTAIN G. F. STIEPANOV
Saturday, April 21, 1956, 21.00 hours

Portsmouth shore agent O2SD submitted the following:

Later last night and during today rumours were picked up by several of our informants. These rumours, which originate from higher Naval officers, have it that the mysterious Mr. Smith whom some call Matthew Smith, and some Bernard Smith, is a high-ranking Admiralty Officer from London, who came to Portsmouth to supervise Crabb's operations. These sources know that Crabb is missing and do not rule out that he may be drowned. But no search has as yet been ordered. The whole affair is clearly being treated with the utmost secrecy.

It appears that the Naval Authorities have ordered the police to take the necessary measures to ensure complete secrecy. This assumption is strengthened by the fact that a Detective Inspector Lamport of the Portsmouth Police today called at the Sallyport Hotel and cut out from the hotel register the four pages containing the names of Commander Crabb and Mr. Smith. The detective also warned the hotel staff not to talk to anyone about the whole matter if they wanted to escape serious trouble.

After having submitted his report, O2SD suggested that I should tell Crabb about the information obtained as this might induce him to speak. But I could not comply with this request, because the prisoner is heavily drugged and in a deep sleep, and Medical Officer Yeremenko stated that the man could not possibly regain consciousness before tomorrow morning. So I ordered Medical Officer Yeremenko to notify me as soon as the prisoner is able to understand what I say and is also able to speak.

Medical Officer Yeremenko's report states that the prisoner's condition is good and that he is being regularly artificially fed. The continuous drugging has as yet not done any harm to his body.

Portsmouth shore agent O23D will submit his next report tomorrow night.

Coded version of this report radioed to headquarters at 22.48 hours, 21.4.1956.

Acknowledgement received at 23.29 hours 21.4.1956, reading:

"KOMORD 2248 HOURS 21/4/1956 RECEIVED—
MOSKOM"
Signed: Capt. G. F. Stiepanov.
Report read: Rear-Admiral V. F. Kotov.

REPORT FROM CAPTAIN G. F. STIEPANOV
Sunday, April 22, 1956. 23.00 hours.

At 08.15 hours Medical Officer Yeremenko notified me that the prisoner had fully recovered consciousness and was able to understand and speak, though he still stubbornly refused to utter a single word to Yeremenko or to the guards. Together with Political Officer Vosensky and Intelligence Officers Shcherkin and Dmitriev, I went to see the prisoner who looked at us searchingly through his bandages.

Told him that we know the identity of his friend who posed as "Smith", that we also now know the identity of the men who sent him to Portsmouth to carry out his underwater examinations of the *Ordzhonikidze*, and ended:

"You know now that your secrets are no secrets to us. I am therefore telling you in all friendliness that it is no use your continuing this foolish silence. If you persist in behaving as you have done up till now, I shall have to consider having you rubbed-out and allow your people to find your body. But if you stop your resistance and answer my questions, it will only be to your advantage. So, do you admit that you are the British Naval frogman Commander Lionel Crabb?"

The prisoner shut his eyes and remained silent. He had not fallen asleep, as ascertained by Medical Officer Yeremenko but had obviously shut his eyes to show that he was not willing to speak. Seeing that the prisoner was determined not to co-operate, I made it clear to him that he had only himself to blame for any consequences and ordered Medical Officer

Yeremenko to inject him again. This order was complied with at once.

Portsmouth shore agent O2SD submitted the following:

Have now received information which confirms the earlier statement that Commander Crabb has been working for the United States Naval Intelligence, under orders to find out details of the *Ordzhonikidze's* hull, so as to throw light on the secret why the cruiser is so easily manoeuvrable, and also to inspect the special anti-submarine and anti-mine radar devices. It has also been confirmed that the Crabb expedition was known to the British Admiralty, who decided that it had officially nothing to do with the affair, and accordingly did not stop the operation. The reason for this unusual strategy was, as our informant discovered, that the Admiralty hoped to share in the secret information obtained. In order to ensure that Crabb's findings were received before the Americans could get them, the Naval Officer, "Smith", was sent from London to Portsmouth, to speak to Crabb when he returned from his underwater expedition.

Other informants state that Naval circles in Portsmouth know about Crabb's disappearance. They are convinced that Crabb died and assume that his oxygen supply failed. Some Naval officers who are Crabb's friends criticise the Naval authorities for not having made any attempt to search for their missing colleague. No one has expressed the opinion or suggestion that Crabb was spotted by our watch and captured, which is clear proof that our swimmers were not observed. Our informants are continuously at work and do their utmost to obtain further information.

Coded version of this report radioed to headquarters at 00.35 hours, 23.4.1956.

Acknowledgement received at 01.27 hours 23.4.1956, reading:

"KOMORD 0035 HOURS 23/4/1956 RECEIVED— MOSKOM"

Signed: Capt. G. F. Stiepanov.

Report read: Rear-Admiral V. F. Kotov.

REPORT FROM CAPTAIN G. F. STIEPANOV
Monday, April 23, 1956. 21.50 hours.

Portsmouth shore agent O2SD submitted the following:

Because of the refusal by the Naval Authorities to search the harbour for the missing frogman, discontent is spreading among those officers and men who personally know Commander Crabb. Some members of H.M.S. *Vernon* are even considering searching the water on their own initiative, believing that their dead comrade's body lies entangled somewhere in the mud. Others express the opinion that it is too late to search for Crabb, because by now the tide will probably have taken the body out into the Channel. According to our investigations, no decision has as yet been reached by these individual rebellious officers and men, but it appears to be a fact that the Naval authorities are definitely not going to do anything in the matter. Our informants are kept continuously on the job, in case of further developments.

We are also pursuing our investigations to obtain conclusive proof that the underwater examination was ordered by United States Naval Intelligence, but though our comrades are working unceasingly on the job they have not up till now managed to establish more than that which we already know.

Since I was not aware that no unexpected action by the British Naval authorities was likely, I considered ordering the relaxation of the continuous drugging of the prisoner, in order to prevent his memory being affected. I ascertained from Medical Officer Yeremenko that in the case of urgency the prisoner could be effectively re-drugged within 15 minutes, and ordered that the injections should cease.

Saw prisoner at 16.45 hours and again attempted to make him speak. But as on previous occasions, all attempts which I, Political Officer Vosensky, and Intelligence Officer Dmitriev made, met with failure. The prisoner simply shuts his eyes and lies in his bed as though dead. When I informed him that, for the time being, the injections would cease, he did not seem to be interested in what I said. Though he is now able to feed himself, he persistently refuses food and drink and has to be continuously forcibly fed.

Coded version of this report radioed to head-quarters at 23.05 hours, 23.4.1956.

Acknowledgement received at 00.20 hours, 24.4.1956, reading:

"KOMORD 2305 HOURS 23/4/1956 RECEIVED—MOSKOM"

Signed: Capt. G. F. Stiepanov.
Report read: Rear-Admiral V. F. Kotov.

REPORT FROM CAPTAIN G. F. STIEPANOV

Tuesday, April 24, 1956. 20.25 hours.

Portsmouth shore agent O2SD submitted the following:

No further information received, our informants are, however, continuing their work.

Prisoner is fully conscious. He still does not speak a single word to Medical Officer Yeremenko or his guards and lies on his bed as though sleeping. Refuses food and drink as before and is forcibly fed.

Coded version of this report radioed to headquarters at 21.00 hours, 24.4.1956.

Acknowledgement received at 21.58 hours 24.4.1956, reading:

"KOMORD 2100 HOURS 24/4/1956 RECEIVED—MOSKOM"

Signed: Capt. G. F. Stiepanov.

Report read: Rear-Admiral V. F. Kotov.

REPORT FROM CAPTAIN G. F. STIEPANOV

Wednesday, April 25, 1956. 21.40 hours.

Portsmouth shore agent O2SD submitted the following:

News about the disappearance of Commander Crabb is now spreading beyond Portsmouth Navy circles, despite the Naval Authorities' stringent secrecy measures. Newspapermen have started to make inquiries about what lies behind the rumours, but the staff of the Sallyport Hotel acts in strict accordance with the detective's warning. Scores of Naval security officers are in the public houses to prevent anything being said. This move strengthens the conclusion that the Naval Authorities have firmly decided not to start any investigation into the Crabb affair.

Our informants have established that those Naval personnel who two days ago were prepared to search the harbour on their own account have given up their plans. This sudden change of plan may be due to pressure having been brought on them by Naval Authorities. Confirmation of this assumption could not be obtained because our informants have to go about with the greatest care, to avoid suspicion. They are all kept continuously on the job.

Further information has been obtained that Crabb worked for United States Naval Intelligence. It has also been established that on various occasions Crabb went to the American Naval Command in London, and his last visit was on April 16. He received his orders from Mr. Jones, as was established from telephone-call records, but it is believed that this is a cover name.

It has now also been established that Crabb told friends in London before his departure for Portsmouth that he was going to do a job on the Russian cruiser and that he hoped to get at least as much information as when he examined the *Sverdlov* during her visit to Portsmouth.

The prisoner behaves as before, does not speak a single word, lies or sits on his bed, persistently refuses food and drink and has to be forcibly fed.

Coded version of this report radioed to headquarters at 23.01 hours, 25.4.1956.

Acknowledgement received at 00.32 hours, 26.4.56, reading:

"KOMORD 2301 HOURS 25/4/1956 RECEIVED—MOSKOM"

Signed: Capt. G. F. Stiepanov.

Report read: Rear-Admiral V. F. Kotov.

REPORT FROM CAPTAIN G. F. STIEPANOV
Thursday, April 26, 1956. 20.00 hours.

Portsmouth shore agent O2SD submitted the following:

Our informants have been unable to glean additional information, they continue their work.

Prisoner behaves exactly as before.

Coded version of this report radioed to headquarters at 20.42 hours, 26.4.1956.

Acknowledgement received at 21.39 hours, 26.4.1946, reading:

"KOMORD 2042 HOURS 26/4/1956 RECEIVED—MOSKOM"

Signed: Capt. G. F. Stiepanov.

Report read: Rear-Admiral V. F. Kotov.

REPORT FROM CAPTAIN G. F. STIEPANOV
Friday, April 27, 1956. 22.30 hours.

Portsmouth shore agent O2SD submitted the following:

Received instructions to stop further investigations into Crabb matter due to your departure tomorrow. Informants obtained further confirmation from entirely different sources, but the new information does not add anything to the known facts, it merely confirms previous reports.

Because of our departure tomorrow, ordered Medical Officer Yeremenko to inject prisoner again. Order has been carried out and prisoner is unconscious.

Coded version of this report radioed to headquarters at 23.18 hours, 27.4.1956.

Acknowledgement received at 00.33 hours, 28.4.1956, reading:

"KOMORD 2318 HOURS 27/4/1956 RECEIVED—MOSKOM"

Signed: Capt. G. F. Stiepanov.

Report read: Rear-Admiral V. F. Kotov.

REPORT FROM CAPTAIN G. F. STIEPANOV
Saturday, April 28, 1956. 23.10 hours.

After leaving British waters, relaxed safety precautions as no more watching by individual sailors in connection with having a prisoner on board appeared necessary. Security officer's report states that crew is aware of our carrying prisoner but unaware of his identity.

Received at 21.01 hours, 28.4.1956, following coded radio message:

"HELICOPTER WILL TAKE PRISONER EARLY 29/4/1956 STOP KEEP DRUG READY FOR IMMEDIATE CLEARANCE—MOSCOM"

Acknowledged message receipt at 21.09 hours, 28.4.1956.

Received at 22.07 hours, 28.4.1956, following coded radio message from Air Command Stettin:

"PREPARING MEETING 0600 HOURS 29/4/1956 STOP PILOT CALLSIGN SSK STOP NEXT COMMUNICATION FROM PILOT—SCEKOM"

Acknowledged message receipt at 22.20 hours, 28.4.1956.

All necessary preparations made.

Coded version of this report radioed to headquarters at 23.57 hours. 28.4.1956. Acknowledgement received at 00.43 hours, 29.4.1956, reading:

"KOMORD 2357 HOURS 28/4/1956 RECEIVED— MOSKOM"

Signed: Capt. G. F. Stiepanov.

REPORT FROM CAPTAIN G. F. STIEPANOV
Sunday, April 29, 1956. 06.45 hours.

Received at 05.15 hours, 29.4.1956, the following coded message from Air Command Stettin:

"SSK ESTIMATED TIME OF ARRIVAL 0620 HOURS PREPARE FOR IMMEDIATE CLEARANCE—SCEKOM"

Acknowledged message receipt at 05.25 hours, 29.4.1956, and confirmed that all arrangements had been made.

Received at 06.28 hours, 29.4.1956, following radio message:

"SSK CALLING EXPECT MEETING EIGHT MINUTES —SSK"

Brought drugged prisoner, tied hand and feet and wrapped in grey blanket, up on deck, plus all his belongings, taken from him when captured, to be ready for hand-over as soon as helicopter arrives.

At 06.35 hours helicopter hovered over foredeck, and lowered basket. Prisoner and his belongings were immediately transferred to this basket and hauled into hovering helicopter. At 06.36 hours, operation completed.

Coded version of this report radioed to headquarters at 07.00 hours, 29.4.1956.

Acknowledgement received at 07.28 hours, 29.4.1956, reading:

"KOMORD 0700 HOURS 29/4/1956 RECEIVED—MOSKOM"

Signed: Capt. G. F. Stiepanov.

REPORT FROM COLONEL ILYUSHIN, CHIEF SECURITY
OFFICER, STETTIN AIR COMMAND

Sunday, April 29, 1956, 08.18 hours.

Airfield cleared according to instructions. From 07.30 hours only our ground staff and security officers present.

SSK landed at base at 08.03 hours. Transferred sleeping prisoner, bound and wrapped in grey blanket, into waiting machine, together with Red Cross box containing his belongings, and with six state security officers who had been ordered to supervise the operation. Ordered Pilot Lieutenant E. N.

Blagodarov to proceed to Minsk, where he was expected and where he was to refuel his machine.

Lieutenant Blagodarov took off at 08.14 hours. Advised Minsk Air Command accordingly.

Signed: Col. A. M. Ilyushin.

REPORT FROM LIEUTENANT- COLONEL O. A. LEBEDIEV, CHIEF SECURITY OFFICER, MINSK AIR COMMAND

Sunday, April 29, 1956. 13.40 hours.

Received at 08.18 hours message from Air Command Chief Security Officer, Stettin, that Lieutenant Blagodarov took off for Minsk at 08.14 hours. Ordered Radio Officer E. S. Pyatiakova to maintain continuous contact with Blagodarov's radio operator. Radio contact maintained every 15 minutes.

According to instructions, cleared airfield at 12.00 hours. Only security officers and ground staff present.

Lieutenant Blagodarov landed his machine at 12.09 hours. Reported slight irregularity of starboard engine. Engineers checked and adjusted engine. Declared machine airworthy at 13.19 hours. Refuelled machine and ordered Lieutenant Blagodarov to proceed to Vnukovo Airport.

Saw prisoner after arrival and before departure. Slept heavily, breathing and pulse normal. Accompanying security officers reported that prisoner was in same condition as when taken on board aircraft.

Lieutenant Blagodarov took off at 13.31 hours. Advised Vnukovo accordingly.

Signed: Lieut.-Col. O. A. Lebediev.

BERICHT VON OBERSTLEUTNANT A.O.LEBEDJEFF,HAUPTSICHERHEITS=

OFFIZIER FLUGKOMMANDO MINSK.

Sonntag,den 29.April 1956. 13,40 Uhr.

Erhielt um 08,18 Uhr Funkspruch vom Hauptsicherheitsoffi=
zier,Flugkommando Stettin,daß Leutnant Blagodaroff um 08,14
Uhr Kurs Minsk abgeflogen ist. Ordnete Funkoffizier E.S.
Pjatjakowa an ständige Funkverbindung mit Blagodaroffs
Funkoperateur zu unterhalten. Funkverbindung 15=minütig un=
terhalten.

Habe gemäß erhaltener Anweisungen.Flugplatz um 12,00 Uhr
geräumt. Habe ausshließlich Sicherheitsoffiziere und Flug=
personal zurückbehalten.

Leutnant Blagodaroff landete seine Maschine um 12,09 Uhr.
Meldete unwesentliche Unregelmäßigkeit des steuerbord Motors.
Dieser wurde von Mechanikern überprüft und in Ordnung ge=
bracht. Maschine um 13,19 Uhr als flugfähig erklärt. Versah
Maschine mit Betriebsstoff und ordnete Leutnant Blagodaroff
an Kurs Wnukowo Flugpaltz weiterzufliegen.

Sah den Gefangenen bei seiner Ankunft und vor dem Abflug.
Die begleitenden Sicherheitsbeamten meldeten,daß der Gefan=
gene im selben Zustand war wie im Augenblick als er an Bord
des Flugzeuges genommen wurde.

Leutnant Blagodaroff flug um 13,31 Uhr ab. Benachrichtigte
Wnukowo demgemäß.

Gez.: Oberstleutnant O.A.Lebedjeff.

Photograph of page from the Secret *Dossier*. Report from Lt.-Col.
A. O. Lebedyev.

There is an error in the document. In the top line the name is
stated as A. O. Lebedyev, but the bottom line says O. A. Lebedyev.

BERICHT VON MAJOR BORIS MARKOWITSCH SMIRNOFF,BESONDERES

KOMMANDO,STAATS SICHERHEITS AUSSCHUß.

Donnerstag,den 6.Juni 1957. 09,30 Uhr.

Unterseeboot Hauptquartier meldete um 00,31 Uhr,daß am 5.
Juni,um 23,40 Uhr eine chiffrierte Funkmeldung von Hauptsicherheitsoffizier Kapitän A.G.Muraloff,an Bord des Un-
terseeflaggschiffes,empfangen wurde,besagend:

„GEMÄß UNSERER DETAILLIERTEN SEEKARTEN NÄHERN WIR UNS DER
STELLE VON DER DIE STRÖMUNG DIE LADUNG HÖCHSTWAHRSCHEINLICH
NAHE PORTSMOUTH ANSCHWEMMEN MAG = PODKOM"

Unterseeboot Hauptquartier meldete am 6.Juni 1957,um 01,26
Uhr den Empfang einer zweiten chiffrierten Funkmeldung von
Hauptsicherheitsoffizier Kapitän Muraloff,an Bord des Un-
terseeflaggschiffes,besagend:

„LADUNG UM 00,59 UHR ABGESANDT STOP SEEKARTEN UND STRÖMUNG
WEISEN AUF ANKUNFT IN 48 STUNDEN HIN = PODKOM"

Gez.: Major B.M.Smirnoff.
Bericht gelesen: Oberst A.P.Mjasskoff.

Photograph of page from the Secret *Dossier*. Report from Maj.
B. M. Smirnov. Translation on page 164.

REPORT FROM MAJOR GALINSKY, CHIEF STATE
SECURITY OFFICER, MOSCOW SPECIAL COMMAND

Sunday, April 29, 1956. 18.19 hours.

While Lieutenant Blagodarov taxied at Vnukovo Airport at 17.24 hours, ordered driver to follow taxiing aircraft in black duty ZIS-car 019. When machine stopped, took prisoner off. He appeared to be slowly regaining consciousness. He was placed between duty sergeants on back seats. Prisoner's belongings, carried in Red Cross box, locked into boot. Ordered driver to proceed direct to Khimky Naval Intelligence Station.

During journey Sergeant Mavshin reported that prisoner was rapidly regaining consciousness. Gradually began to look out of window at me and then at driver. Ordered duty sergeants to untie his hands and feet. When this was done, prisoner remained in same position as before and did not even attempt to stretch himself.

On arrival at Naval Intelligence Station, duty officer ordered me to take prisoner, who had regained complete consciousness, to interrogation room. Prisoner was able to walk. Did not make any attempt to feign inability.

In interrogation room, duty officer ordered guard to bring dungarees for prisoner, who was still wearing pyjamas. Prisoner was able to put on the dungarees and slippers. While he was dressing, a guard brought a plate of hot Borshch. Prisoner pushed it away and remained stiffly seated in his chair, looking straight in front of him.

At 18.12 hours Investigation Judge Colonel I. S. Zhabotin entered interrogation room. Formally handed over prisoner and his belongings.

Signed: Major L. A. Galinsky.

TRANSCRIPT FROM TAPE-BAND, RECORDED FROM INTERROGATION ROOM ON SUNDAY, APRIL 29, 1956, 18.14 HOURS. RECORDING IN ENGLISH, OFFICIAL TRANSLATION. INVESTIGATION JUDGE COLONEL IVAN SEMYONOVICH ZHABOTIN INTERROGATES PRISONER —ENGLISH NAVAL COMMANDER LIONEL CRABB

Colonel Zhabotin: "Go on, eat, Commander Crabb. We want you to feel comfortable here." (63 seconds' silence.) "Don't sit here yawning and staring in front of you, Crabb.

"Eat, relax." (30 seconds' pause. Colonel Zhabotin orders in Russian over intercom telephone): "Bring him some strong coffee to wake him up." (Continues in English): "Do you admit that you are the British Naval Commander Lionel Crabb?" (40 seconds' silence. Colonel Zhabotin continues): "Now, look here, we know everything——"

Crabb (in a quiet voice): "If you know everything, why do you ask me?"

Colonel Zhabotin: "Because we want to hear from you what you have to say."

Crabb: "Well, I have nothing to say."

Colonel Zhabotin (in friendly voice): "I would not advise you to take this attitude. We do not seek to squeeze secrets out of you. All we want is to have a friendly discussion with you so that we can re-check our facts. But if you persist in your foolish attitude, I can assure you we have also ways and means of making you talk."

(At this moment a guard brought in the coffee, which Commander Crabb drank without much persuasion.*)

Colonel Zhabotin: "That's right, drink the black coffee, Commander. It's nice and strong and will wake you up." (28 seconds' pause.) "Go on, drink it. It's a good aromatic brew." (9 seconds' pause.) "That's better. Did you enjoy it?"

Crabb: "Thank you."

Colonel Zhabotin: "Now, what about confirming that you are the British Naval Commander Lionel Crabb?" (21 seconds' silence. Colonel Zhabotin continues): "Go on, confirm it. You see that we know who you are, otherwise I wouldn't call you by your rank and name. So why not admit it?"

Crabb: "If you are so sure that I am who you say I am, there is no need for me to say anything."

Colonel Zhabotin: "Your way of thinking amuses me, Commander. You haven't once tried to deny that you are you, but you won't formally confirm your identity. I could force you to do so, but I have no such intentions. Besides, your non-denial actually

---

* In the transcript this is stated as follows:
A knock. Colonel Zhabotin (in Russian): "Enter." Opening of door. Steps. Colonel Zhabotin (in Russian): "Put the coffee on the table and bring a meal." Guard (in Russian): "Very well." Steps. Shutting of door.

amounts to an admission, and for the moment . . ."

(At this moment a guard brought in the meal.*)

Colonel Zhabotin: "Here you have a real Russian dish: bef-stroganov, and kysel for an after. Bon appetit, Commander."

(4.52 minutes' noise of eating and of dishes being put away.)

Colonel Zhabotin: "Did you enjoy your meal?"

Crabb: "Thank you."

Colonel Zhabotin: "Now, what about confirming that you are the British Naval Commander Lionel Crabb?" (22 seconds' silence. Colonel Zhabotin continues): "Listen, Commander, I want to help you, I don't want to pump you for valuable information. But if I am to help you, you must drop your silly attitude and must help me to help you. It may sound strange to you that despite your despicable spying expedition in Stokes Bay I should want to help you instead of passing you right away to the tribunal for sentence on charges of espionage. But we Russians are not after blood, especially not if we know that we have only caught a tool who has merely acted on orders from his superiors. So, perhaps you will now see reason and be more communicative than before. As I have already said, we have proof that you are the famous British Naval Commander Lionel Crabb, also known as Buster Crabb. If you so wish, you can have sight of the *dossier*, about yourself, which

* In the transcript this is given as follows:
A knock. Colonel Zhabotin (in Russian): "Enter." Opening of door. Steps. Colonel Zhabotin (in Russian): "Put the food on the table." Noise of tray being put down. Steps, closing of door.

includes not only extensive data about you, but also some most interesting photographs."

(17 seconds' silence.)

Crabb: "I am Lionel Crabb. But I am a freelance frogman and have not worked for the Admiralty for quite a time."

Colonel Zhabotin: "I am glad that you have listened to my advice and are beginning to co-operate." (3½ seconds' silence. Colonel Zhabotin continues): "You say that you have not worked for your Admiralty for quite a time. That may or may not be so. But you attempted to survey the hull of the cruiser *Ordzhonikidze* for the American Naval Intelligence, did you not?"

Crabb: "No, I did not."

Colonel Zhabotin: "I know otherwise. I also know the true identity of the man who called himself Bernard and Matthew Smith. But let's forget this question for the moment. What, then, is your story of why you went to examine the hull of the cruiser *Ordzhonikidze*?"

Crabb: "Out of mere personal interest." (3¼ seconds' silence. Crabb continues): "Having heard and read a lot about the striking manoeuvring abilities of the cruiser, and being highly interested in Naval constructions, I fell to the temptation."

Colonel Zhabotin: "You really want me to believe such a story, Commander?"

Crabb: "I do not ask you to believe anything. I have merely told you the truth."

Colonel Zhabotin: "And I tell you that you went to examine the *Ordzhonikidze's* hull on orders from

American Naval Intelligence. I am making this definite statement on account of extensive investigations which have been made in this matter. You would be surprised if you knew how much information we have about the whole affair."

Crabb: "All I can say is that you must have wrong information. You asked me to give you my side of the story, so I am telling you the true facts."

Colonel Zhabotin: "I appreciate your British code of honour, Commander. I even understand that as a British Naval Officer you would prefer to take the blame for your action, rather than involve your superiors. But permit me to tell you that as far as your own Admiralty is concerned, you are already a dead man for them. Your Admiralty today announced that Commander Crabb is presumed dead as a result of certain underwater trials in Stokes Bay."

Crabb: "Does not this announcement confirm that they did not and do not know anything about me?"

Colonel Zhabotin: "On the contrary. It destroys your story that the Admiralty does not know anything about your expedition. If it were true that you went to the *Ordzhonikidze* out of mere private interest, and without the knowledge of your Admiralty, or any other admiralty, how do you explain the presence of the senior Naval officer posing as Smith? But apart from this important fact, if your story were true and your Admiralty had no knowledge of your espionage attempts, how then can they today announce that you died as a result of certain underwater trials in Stokes Bay? Listen to what your

Admiralty has announced: 'Commander Crabb is presumed to be dead as a result of trials with certain underwater apparatus. The location was in Stokes Bay, and it is nine days since the accident.' Seeing now how things are, it is only in your own interest if you revoke your previous story and tell me the down-to-earth facts, Commander Crabb."

Crabb: "All I can tell you is that what I have told you is true." (2 seconds' silence. Crabb continues): "But how do I know that the Admiralty really made this announcement? *Reuter's* report from London, which you showed me, could easily have been faked."

Colonel Zhabotin: "You must take my word for it."

Crabb: "Then you must take my word for what I tell you."

Colonel Zhabotin (in a more pronounced but still quiet voice): "I must warn you, Commander Crabb, that it is not our practice to allow prisoners whom we have caught in the actual act of spying to try to play cat and mouse with us. You surely realise the serious position in which you are placed, and doubtless know that in our country military espionage is punishable by the supreme penalty. Also, in your particular case, no one will lift a finger to try to help you, because your Admiralty has already pronounced you dead."

(62 seconds' silence.)

Colonel Zhabotin: "You have already admitted that you are the famous British Naval Commander Lionel Crabb. For the purposes of record, I want you now to confirm that it was American Naval Intelligence which employed you to carry out the examination of the *Ordzhonikidze's* hull. And I must make it clear to you that your confirmation of facts already obtained by us does not worsen your position at all; on the contrary, it greatly helps you."

Crabb: "I cannot help you there. All I can do is to confirm that what I did was done out of purely personal interest."

Colonel Zhabotin (in a louder voice): "This stubborn renewal of your poor fairytale won't get you far, Commander. We have ways and means of making our prisoners talk. If we so wish, we can inject you with drugs which make you speak the truth. After having got all the information from you which we need, we can let you rot away in prison, or we can shoot you. But we can also reward you, that is, if you co-operate with us. It is thus entirely up to you to choose your own fate."

Crabb (sounding ironical): "I thank you for your kind explanation. But I have already said what there is to be said and I do not intend to invent imaginary tales."

Colonel Zhabotin: "Then there is no use in continuing our conversation. Before I dismiss you, I must tell you, however, that not only have we conclusive proof that you attempted to spy on the *Ordzhonikidze* for American Naval Intelligence, and that your own Admiralty was to share in your discoveries, but we have also complete evidence that this was not your first attempt to spy on our vessels while in British waters. We have conclusive evidence that you did this sort of thing before, that you carried out underwater spying examinations in our cruiser *Sverdlov* when it lay at anchor at Portsmouth when on a friendly visit to England, and that in fact you managed to get away with it." (2¾ seconds' silence. Colonel Zhabotin continues): "Now, knowing that we are fully aware of everything you did, you may perhaps find sufficient time to think about whether you wish to co-operate with me or not, while in prison." (Ordering over the intercom telephone): "Take over the prisoner."

END OF TRANSCRIPT FROM TAPE-BAND.

REPORT FROM PRISON OFFICER SERGEANT
R. P. YANOVIAK
Sunday, April 29, 1956. 20.55 hours.

Took over prisoner at 20.00 hours from duty officer at Naval Intelligence Station, Khimky, and escorted him handcuffed to closed prison van. During journey prisoner sat still, did not reply to anything I said and also refused Papirosi which I offered him. Proceeded to Lefortovo Prison. Handed prisoner over to commandant, Colonel G. G. Zuskin, at 20.44 hours.

Signed: Sgt. R. P. Yanoviak.
Report read: Col. I. S. Zhabotin.

REPORT FROM LIEUTENANT-COLONEL GRIGORI GRIGORYEVICH ZUSKIN, COMMANDANT OF LEFORTOVO PRISON
Sunday, April 29, 1956. 22.30 hours.

At 20.10 hours Investigation Judge Colonel I. S. Zhabotin telephoned me from Naval Intelligence

Station, Khimky. He informed me of the special nature of the prisoner and requested me to make arrangements whereby the prisoner can be questioned at any time of the day or night, and also to have an interpreter at hand because the prisoner is an Englishman.

At 20.44 hours Sergeant R. P. Yanoviak handed over to me prisoner, whom he brought in from Naval Intelligence Station, Khimky. I told prisoner, with the help of Interpreter Olga Vasilyevna Dubchinskaya, that this is not a sanatorium but a prison and that nonsense of any kind would not be tolerated. When I asked the prisoner whether he understood, he did not answer. And when I asked his name, etc., he did not reply either. My threatening him with disciplinary action if he continues his attitude did not help. So all I could do was to make it clear to him that he had lost his identity anyway and that from now on he was no more than No. 147.

Because of the special nature of the case I accommodated the prisoner in the isolation block. Assigned interpreter Dubchinskaya to the guards of the isolation block, because none of them speaks or understands English.

Though the prisoner persistently refuses to answer any question, or even to reply to any remark made to him, he does not give trouble. When taken to his cell and told that he could lie down, he at once complied, but turned his back to me. In accordance with instructions received, made it clear to the guards that even if the prisoner provokes or attacks them, no violence must take place, and warned them that whoever lost his head would mercilessly be brought before the tribunal for sentence.

Re-checked tape-recording system in the interrogation cell and found it in perfect working order.

Signed: Lt.-Col. G. G. Zuskin.

Report read: Col. I. S. Zhabotin.

REPORT FROM CAPT. K. F. NIKOLAYEV

Monday, April 30, 1956. 03.45 hours.

Arrived at Lefortovo Prison at 01.50 hours. Ordered the prisoner to be brought to interrogation cell. Prisoner was brought in at 02.01 hours. He appeared sleepy but alert.

TRANSCRIPT FROM TAPE-RECORDING—OFFICIAL TRANSLATION FROM ENGLISH:

Capt. Nikolayev: "Commander Crabb, will you tell me why you went to Portsmouth to carry out the underwater examination of the cruiser *Ordzhonikidze*?"

Crabb: "Out of mere personal interest."

Capt. Nikolayev: "You told this to Colonel Zhabotin who did not accept your tale. You don't expect me to believe you, do you?"

Crabb: "I do not expect anything, I am simply telling you why I did it."

Capt. Nikolayev: "Why not come clean and admit that you did it for United States Naval Intelligence in London?"

Crabb: "I can't admit to something which is not the truth."

Capt. Nikolayev: "We have conclusive proof that

what we say is a fact. Whether you admit it or not, we have foolproof evidence."

Crabb: "Why then do you insist on my admitting it?"

Capt. Nikolayev: "We want it for purposes of the record."

Crabb: "I still regret to being unable to confirm something which is not true."

Capt. Nikolayev: "So, let me tell you we have conclusive proof that you went to the United States Naval Intelligence in London on April 16, and that Mr. Jones gave you your instructions as to what to do in Portsmouth."

Crabb: "All I can say is that you have the wrong proof."

Capt. Nikolayev: "Are you determined to keep to your story?"

Crabb: "It's not a question of being determined, it's a question of speaking the truth."

Captain Nikolayev: "Let's drop this point for the moment. Perhaps you will now tell me something about your friend who posed as Smith?"

Crabb: "What is the use of telling you something that you don't believe anyway?"

Capt. Nikolayev: "If you speak the truth we shall believe you. We have extensive information on the matter and are thus able to check on what extent you are speaking the truth. So what can you tell me about your friend who called himself Smith?"

Crabb: "He is an old friend of mine. We served together in the Navy during the war and have a lot in common."

Capt. Nikolayev: "I am not interested in the past, I want to know the real name of your friend."

Crabb: "His name is Smith."

Capt. Nikolayev: "What's his first name?"

Crabb: "Matthew."

Capt. Nikolayev: "Now I have caught you. Your friend chose the name of Bernard in the Sallyport Hotel register."

Crabb: "That's his second name."

Capt. Nikolayev: "Listen, Commander, that's enough. We know that Smith is not his real name. We also know what he does in Whitehall. But we want to hear it from you. So, firstly, what does he do?"

Crabb: "He has a tobacconist's shop...."

Capt. Nikolayev (voice raised): "I won't allow you to make a fool out of me. If you think you can pull my leg, I will show you who calls the tune here. So, will you tell me now what your friend does?"

Crabb: "I told you but you don't believe me."

Capt. Nikolayev: "I'll give you another chance, but if you insist on continuing as you have done up till now, you will be sorry. So, tell me now what you discovered when you made your successful underwater examination of the cruiser *Sverdlov* when she visited England?"

Crabb: "Nothing. The whole thing was a false alarm."

Capt. Nikolayev: "What do you mean by false alarm?"

Crabb: "Someone informed the police that anti-Communist refugees had planted an underwater time-bomb under the cruiser *Sverdlov*, to blow her up. To prevent any incident, volunteers were called to make sure that the security of the cruiser was not impaired. I was picked, because of my wartime experience in this field and I searched the *Sverdlov*. Nothing was found and so I returned to base."

Capt. Nikolayev: "I must admit that you are very good at inventing tales, Commander Crabb. But I am not impressed, I don't like fiction. I want facts and nothing but facts. And the facts are that you surveyed the cruiser for United States Naval Intelligence in London. Do you admit it?"

Crabb: "I do not."

Capt. Nikolayev: "I have proof that you did."

Crabb: "You seem to have proof for any fantastic allegation."

Capt. Nikolayev: "That's enough now. I'll let you rot away in your prison cell. I'll teach you how to behave. Not only spying on our ships but being impertinent on top of it, is too much. You'll find this out for yourself soon enough."

(END OF TRANSCRIPT FROM TAPE-BAND.)

Ordered to escort prisoner to his cell.

Signed: Captain. K. F. Nikolayev.

Report read: Col. I. S. Zhabotin.

REPORT FROM LIEUTENANT-COLONEL GRIGORI GRIGORYEVICH ZUSKIN

Monday, April 30, 1956. 16.30 hours.

Saw prisoner at 06.00 hours. He was sound asleep when I and Interpreter Dubchinskaya entered his cell. Had to shake him to awaken him. He imme-

diately rose from his bunk, probably presuming that
he was to be interrogated again.

Told him with the help of Interpreter Dubchinskaya that due to his defiance his food will consist of
stale bread and jugs of lukewarm water, but added
that he would receive normal food and treatment if
he co-operates. The prisoner did not comment and
stood to attention all the time.

Ordered Sgt. O. P. Eykhler to wear prisoner's
physical strength out by subjugating him to
strenuous physical training in the prison yard several
times a day, as this may break his defiant spirit. I
then spoke once more to all guards of the isolation
block and warned them again that under no circumstances was violence to be shown towards the prisoner,
and repeated my previous warning that any disregard
of my orders would be dealt with mercilessly by the
Tribunal.

Sgt. O. P. Eykhler reported to me that from 07.30
to 08.30, from 11.00 to 12.00 and from 14.30 to
15.30 hours he had subjected the prisoner to heavy
physical training in the prison yard. Despite his being
middle-aged, the prisoner is extremely physically fit
and able to carry out any exercise. Further physical
training will be carried out from 17.30 to 18.30 and
from 20.00 to 21.00 hours.

Saw prisoner at 16.00 hours with Interpreter
Dubchinskaya and asked him whether he wished to
see the interrogation officer to make a statement. No
reply received.

Signed: Lt.-Col. G. G. Zuskin.
Report read: Col. I. S. Zhabotin.

REPORT FROM MAJOR T. A. DUBNIKOV
Tuesday, May 1, 1956. 07.15 hours.

Had the prisoner brought before me to the interrogation cell at 22.40 hours, 30.4.1956.

(The report has here the transcript of the taperecording which is identical with that in Capt. Nikolayev's report on page 87 and is therefore not repeated.)

While reading out my questions to the prisoner from the *dossier*, I watched the man to see whether he tried to see what was contained in the *dossier*. But he did not once look towards it. At the end of the interrogation I had the prisoner taken back to his cell.

Had the prisoner brought back to interrogation cell at 00.10 hours, 1.5.1956. Same procedure as at previous interrogation, as shown on tape recording. When I finished, I had him taken back to his cell.

Interrogated prisoner again at 02.30 hours, at 04.05 hours and 05.40 hours. Though prisoner appeared very sleepy, he was mentally alert, and did not protest at his continuously being torn away from his sleep. During these three interrogations, the procedure was the same as before, as is seen from the tape-recordings.

Having watched the prisoner closely each time and having taken into consideration that he is physically worn out, I have come to the conclusion that he either is a perfect liar remembering his answers extremely well, or that he speaks the truth.

Signed: Major T. A. Dubnikov.
Report read: Col. I. S. Zhabotin.

REPORT FROM LIEUTENANT-COLONEL G. G. ZUSKIN

Tuesday, May 1, 1956. 21.45 hours.

Sgt. O. P. Eykhler reported to me that prisoner was subjected to hard physical training from 07.30 to 08.30, from 11.00 to 12.00, from 14.30 to 15.30, from 17.30 to 18.30 and from 20.00 to 21.00 hours. Prisoner carried out orders but since 15.00 hours showed signs of exhaustion, which increased at later exercises.

Duty Sergeant N. N. Mirsky reported that each time the prisoner was brought back to his cell, he fell on his bunk and was at once deeply asleep. He ate only some of his bread and drank very little.

Saw prisoner together with Interpreter Dubchinskaya in his cell at 18.50 hours. I asked him:

"Have you any complaints or wishes?"

For the first time the prisoner spoke and said:

"No, thanks."

I explained to him again that it was entirely up to him to change his present position, and promised him that life would be considerably better for him if he saw reason and decided to co-operate. His reply was:

"I can't do the impossible. Thanks for your interest anyway."

I told him that if he should decide to change his mind, all he had to do is to ask to see me. His reply to this:

"Thanks again."

Medical Officer Dr. K. B. Richter examined the prisoner at 19.20 hours. He reported to me that the prisoner's physical exhaustion is considerable but his strong constitution indicates that the present routine can be continued.

I consequently ordered Sgt. O. P. Eykhler to go on with the agreed schedule until further notice.

Signed: Lieut.-Col. G. G. Zuskin.

Report read: Col. I. S. Zhabotin.

REPORT FROM MAJOR T. A. DUBNIKOV
Wednesday, May 2, 1956. 05.20 hours.

Had the prisoner brought to me in the interrogation cell at 04.15 hours. Looked very tired and worn out.

TRANSCRIPT FROM TAPE-BAND—OFFICIAL TRANSLATION FROM ENGLISH

Major Dubnikov: "Sit down, Commander. How do you feel?"

Crabb: "Thank you, very well."

Major Dubnikov: "What's the use of pretending, Commander? The mere look of you tells me that you feel far from well. Why not admit the truth?"

Crabb: "What truth?"

Major Dubnikov: "The truth about how you really feel."

Crabb: "Why, do you want me to complain?"

Major Dubnikov: "Of course. If you have any complaints to make, tell me. If your complaints are sound, I will take the necessary steps to put matters right. So what do you wish to complain about, Commander?"

Crabb: "Well, I have no complaints."

BERICHT VON KAPITÄN NIKITA ILJITSCH MURJANTZ,OFFIZIER DES

BESONDEREN FORSCHUNGSDIENSTES.

Donnerstag,den 4.April 1957. 23,00 Uhr.

Wendete mich befehlsgemäß an Leutnant L.L.Korabloff. Vorge=
bend seinen gegenwärtigen Namen nicht zu kennen,sprach ich
ihn „Buster" an und sagte ihm,daß ich ihn im Kriege während
meines Dienstes mit den Verbündeten kennengelernt habe. Ich
sprach,wie befohlen,englisch,aber er entgegnete in russischer
Sprache,daß er meine Sprache nicht verstehe und bat mich in
russisch zu wiederholen was ich gesagt hatte. Ich tat es,aber
er sagte,mir fest in die Augen sehend,daß ich ihn mit jemandem,
den ich kennengelernt habe und der ihm ähnlich sieht,verwech=
selt haben müsse.

Ich erwähnte dann einige Einzelheiten über ihn,die im Auskunfts=
blatt enthalten sind,und beobachtete ihn haarscharf als ich
sprach. Seine Augen verrieten jedoch nicht ein einziges Mal,daß
ich über sein früheres Leben sprach. Er bestand erneut darauf,
daß ich mich irre,sagte,daß es ihm leid tue,daß ich den Mann,
den ich offensichtlich gerne finden wolle,nicht gefunden habe,
und lud mich ein mit ihm zu trinken.

Wir tranken 4 Gläser Vodka miteinander,und ich nützte diese Ge=
legenheit aus,über Kriegsepisoden zu sprechen,die im Auskunfts=
blatt enthalten sind. Ich konnte jedoch nurmehr allgemeines In=
teresse in Korabloffs Augen und Gesicht erspähen. Er machte den
Eindruck eines Menschen,der einem Unbekannten,der ihm etwas er=
zählt das er vorher nie gehört hatte,zuhört. Er erweckte auch
den Eindruck,daß er an dem Thema nicht besonders interessiert
war und nur deshalb zuhörte,um gesellig zu erscheinen.

Ich bin überzeugt davon,daß er nicht durchsah,daß ich auftrags=
gemäß handelte,und vorgab ihn während des Krieges kennengelernt
zu haben,um herauszufinden zu versuchen,wie weit er aus sich
herausgehen würde,falls ihn irgendjemand,den er in seinem frü=
heren Leben gekannt hatte,ausfindig machen würde. Sein Benehmen
stellt es klar,daß er mit seinen erfolgreichen Taktiken,die mich
überzeugt haben mußten,daß ich ihn mit jemandem anderen verwech=
selt habe,zufrieden war.

Die Tatsache,daß ich Korabloff vollkommen unversehens und unvor=
bereitet versucht habe zu überrumpeln,und sein Benehmen in einer
solchen Falle,deutet auf die realistische Schlußfolgerung hin,
daß L.L.Korabloff vollkommen vertrauenswürdig ist,und nicht
plant jendwelche Gelegenheit wahrzunehmen,Schutz bei einer Aus=
landsmacht zu suchen.

Gez.: Kapitän N.I.Murjantz.

Bericht gelesen,überaus zufriedenstellend,
Oberst A.P.Mjasskoff.

Photograph of page from the Secret *Dossier*. Report from Captain
N. I. Muryants. Translation on page 157.

The style of this report is very clumsy.

"Buster" Crabb in diving gear.

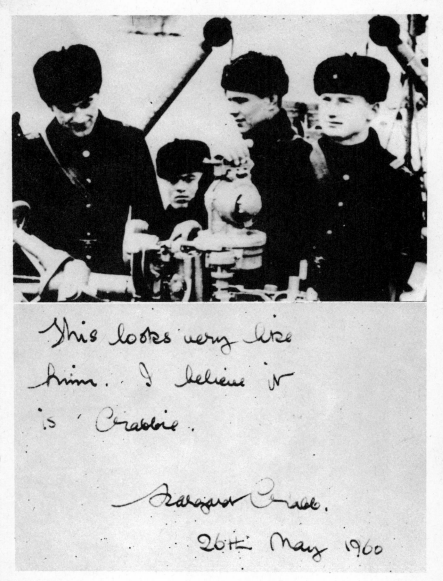

This looks very like him. I believe it is 'Crabbie'.

Margaret Crabb.

26th May 1960

The top photograph was taken in late Autumn 1959 and recently smuggled out of Russia. The officer at the left is said to be Commander Crabb, on board a Russian vessel; he is now serving as First Lieutenant Lev Lvovich Korablov in the Far Eastern Command of the Red Navy at Vladivostok.

When Mrs. Margaret Crabb saw this photograph, she made the statement reproduced below the photo.

Colonel Myaskov, Crabb's chief interrogator.

Major Dubnikov: "Do you mean to say that you consider you are being treated well?"

Crabb: "As well as a man in my position can expect."

Major Dubnikov: "This is not an answer to my question."

Crabb: "It is how things are."

Major Dubnikov: "Why don't you climb down from your high horse and drop your ridiculous conceit? Why not come out into the open and say what's really on your mind? Why not make a clean breast and get things over?"

Crabb: "What do you want me to tell you?"

Major Dubnikov: "The truth."

Crabb: "I have told you, and your colleagues, the truth all along. But you are all obsessed with the idea that I am telling lies. You have questioned me umpteen times and on every single occasion have asked me the same questions. You do your utmost to break me down, in order to make me change my mind. Is it your intention to force me to invent a tale in order to please you, or do you want the truth?"

Major Dubnikov: "We want the truth. But we know that it is not the truth you are telling us."

Crabb: "Here we go again."

Major Dubnikov: "What do you mean?"

Crabb: "You don't believe what I say. When I was captured by your swimmers, I knew that I hadn't a chance. Your constant disbelieving of my words, your questioning and treatment confirms that I am right."

Major Dubnikov: "On the contrary, Commander,

you are very wrong. You look at things with typical
English eyes, you transfer English methods to the
Soviet Union. Let me tell you that, contrary to
English practice, we Russians give anyone a fair
chance. You, too, Commander, will receive fair treatment if you decide to see reason. But if you continue
to tell us packs of lies, then I cannot guarantee anything."

Crabb: "You are convinced that I am refusing to
tell you the truth. Why then don't you simply shoot
me instead of wasting your time and that of your
colleagues on me?"

Major Dubnikov: "It is we, who will decide what
is to be your fate, Commander. Sometimes death is
easier than a certain life, and let me tell you that life
can be still more unpleasant for you than it is now."

Crabb: "I am aware of that."

Major Dubnikov: "So why not answer my
questions instead of going through hell?"

Crabb: "All right, have it your way. Ask me what
you want to know."

Major Dubnikov: "You went into the water in
Portsmouth in order to carry out underwater
examinations of the cruiser *Ordzhonikidze's* hull?"

Crabb: "That is so."

Major Dubnikov: "Prior to the arrival of the
Soviet Naval Squadron in Portsmouth, you negotiated
the possibility of carrying out underwater examinations of the cruiser *Ordzhonikidze*, and possibly of
other of our vessels, with the United States Naval
Intelligence in London?"

Crabb: "You said it."

Major Dubnikov: "On April 16, 1956, you went to see the United States Naval Intelligence in London and received your instructions for your journey to Portsmouth from Mr. Jones?"

Crabb: "You said it."

Major Dubnikov: "We know that the name 'Jones' in the telephone-call records is a cover name for a very high United States official. What is Mr. Jones' real name?"

Crabb: "I don't know."

Major Dubnikov: "You must know. Or do you mean to suggest that the name Jones is unfamiliar to you?"

Crabb: "The name is familiar to me, it is a very common name. But I don't know a Mr. Jones who is an American."

Major Dubnikov: "Then let me put my question in another form: Who is the man who gave you your instructions for your underwater examinations of the *Ordzhonikidze's* hull?"

Crabb: "No one gave me any instructions. It was my own idea."

Major Dubnikov: "Now we are getting further. You say then that it was your own idea and that you offered to the American Naval Intelligence in London that you should carry out underwater examinations of the cruiser *Ordzhonikidze* for them?"

Crabb: "I did not say that. I said it was my own idea."

Major Dubnikov: "All right then. But tell me,

how much was your information worth to Mr. Jones?"

Crabb: "What do you mean?"

Major Dubnikov: "I want to know from you the amount of money which you agreed to accept from the Americans for your underwater examination of the *Ordzhonikidze*."

Crabb: "For Christ's sake, how often do I have to repeat that the whole expedition was my own idea, that I did not carry out the underwater examination for anybody, but that I did it out of mere personal curiosity."

Major Dubnikov: "But you confirmed a little while ago to me that you negotiated the possibility of carrying out underwater examinations of the cruiser *Ordzhonikidze*, and possibly also of other of our vessels, with the United States Naval Intelligence in London."

Crabb: "I did not say anything of the sort. I merely commented on your fantastic story with the words 'you said it'. Wasn't it clear to you what my remark meant?"

Major Dubnikov (voice raised): "Now listen, Commander. Everything has its limits. And you have reached your limit. Under no circumstances will I allow you to lead me up the garden path. You either change your attitude completely, or you . . ."

[Noise of something heavy falling. End of tape transcript.]

The prisoner had passed out. Made sure that he was unconscious and sent for the Medical Officer to come urgently. Dr. K. B. Richter arrived in the interrogation cell eight minutes later and examined the man. He found that the prisoner was genuinely unconscious, probably due to extensive exhaustion.

On Medical Officer's advice, ordered the prisoner's removal to his cell, and sanctioned that prisoner's physical exercises should be cut to three hours a day until further notice.

My opinion, that the prisoner speaks the truth, or at least to a great extent, is strengthened by my observations of his reactions which I made during the interrogation. But due to the prisoner's high intelligence and ability to react to any unforeseen situation, I cannot rule out that he may be an excellent liar thoroughly rehearsed in his role and with a good memory.

Signed: Major T. A. Dubnikov.
Report read: Col. I. S. Zhabotin.

REPORT FROM LIEUTENANT-COLONEL G. G. ZUSKIN
Wednesday, May 2, 1956. 20.30 hours.

Medical Officer Dr. K. B. Richter reported that the prisoner is again fit, though in a notably exhausted state. His last examination of the prisoner was made at 19.15 hours, and he found that the physical training has not harmed the prisoner's constitution but only weakened his general physical condition. He advised, however, that three hours' physical training per day should not be exceeded for the time being.

Sgt. O. P. Eykhler reported that he subjected the prisoner from 09.00 to 10.00, from 13.30 to 14.30, and from 18.00 to 19.00 hours to strenuous physical training. The prisoner complied with every command, but his movements were slower than on previous days, especially during the last exercises. Sgt. Eykhler is impressed by the prisoner's physical fitness and determination, and expresses his doubts that this man will be broken by these otherwise successful methods.

Informed Investigation Judge Col. I. S. Zhabotin over the telephone at 20.10 hours about prisoner's condition and the doctor's opinion and obtained his formal consent to the present schedule.

Signed: Lt.-Col. G. G. Zuskin.

Report read: Col. I. S. Zhabotin.

REPORT FROM LIEUTENANT-COLONEL G. G. ZUSKIN

Thursday, May 3, 1956. 21.00 hours.

Dr. K. B. Richter reported to me that he examined the prisoner at 19.15 hours, 15 minutes after his last physical exercise, and found that his general condition has only slightly weakened. He is, however, of the opinion that this is not due to his being subjected to hard physical training but to his eating only part of the bread which is given daily to him. His heart is in perfect condition and Dr. Richter does not expect that the continuation of the schedule would substantially harm the prisoner's constitution.

Sgt. O. P. Eykhler reported that he subjected the prisoner from 09.00 to 10.00, from 13.30 to 14.30, and from 18.00 to 19.00 hours to hard physical training. The movements of the prisoner are notably slower than the previous day, but he complies with every command and seems to be determined not to show any weakness.

Informed Investigation Judge Col. I. S. Zhabotin over the telephone at 20.49 hours about the prisoner's condition and the doctor's opinion, and obtained his sanction to carry on as at present.

Signed: Lt.-Col. G. G. Zuskin.

Report read: Col. I. S. Zhabotin.

REPORT FROM LIEUTENANT-COLONEL G. G. ZUSKIN

Friday, May 4, 1956. 18.45 hours.

Sgt. N. N. Mirsky reported to me at 07.59 hours that prisoner has been violently sick and that he finds it difficult to get up from his bunk. To my question, whether he suspects that the prisoner feigns illness, Sgt. Mirsky replied that this is definitely not the case but that the prisoner appears genuinely ill. In his opinion the trouble may be due to the prisoner having been given mouldy bread the previous evening, which he ate and parts of which are still in his cell.

I asked Medical Officer Dr. K. B. Richter to see the prisoner and to report his findings to me immediately afterwards. Dr. Richter saw me at 08.23 hours and informed me that he had found signs of slight food poisoning of the prisoner. He stated that though there is no real danger to the prisoner's life, he had nevertheless instructed the Medical Orderly to pump out the stomach and to clean out his whole system. Dr. Richter considers it, however, imperative to stop the bread and water diet and to substitute it

with hospital diet No. 1. He also advises to stop, for
the time being, any physical exercises and to put the
man on the sick list.

I telephoned Investigation Judge Col. I. S.
Zhabotin at 08.35 hours but was advised that he
would be off duty until 10.00 hours, but he would
then contact me. Col. Zhabotin telephoned me back
at 10.09 hours, and I informed him of the exact
position. He agreed to comply exactly with Dr.
Richter's advice, and requested me to report to him
again on the prisoner's condition at 18.30 hours.

Ordered Sgt. O. P. Eykhler to cancel prisoner's
physical exercises until further notice.

Saw prisoner together with Dr. Richter and Interpreter Dubchinskaya at 11.20 hours. He was sound
asleep and Dr. Richter found his breathing regular.
He looks very pale and has visibly lost substantial
weight.

At 12.30 hours Sgt. N. N. Mirsky reported to me
that the Medical Orderly had brought the prisoner
soup, and that he ate it obediently. Having finished
his meal, he lay back on his bunk and fell asleep
almost at once.

At 18.05 hours Dr. Richter reported to me that
he had examined the prisoner at 17.50 hours, just
after he had eaten a plate of Kasha. His condition
is improving but Dr. Richter strongly advises that
we should continue to keep him on the sick list.

Telephoned Investigation Judge Col. I. S.
Zhabotin at 18.30 hours and reported to him the
exact state of affairs concerning the prisoner. He
instructed me to comply with the Medical Officer's

advice and to inform him about the prisoner tomorrow morning at 10.15 hours.

Signed: Lt.-Col. G. G. Zuskin.

Report read: Col. I. S. Zhabotin.

REPORT FROM LIEUTENANT-COLONEL G. G. ZUSKIN

Saturday, May 5, 1956. 18.40 hours.

Dr. K. B. Richter reported to me that at 09.40 hours he thoroughly examined the prisoner and found that his condition has greatly improved. He advises to continue treatment and to keep physical exercises cancelled.

Telephoned Investigation Judge Col. I. S. Zhabotin at 10.15 hours, reported Medical Officer's findings, was ordered by Col. Zhabotin to comply with doctor's orders, and to report to him again at 18.30 hours.

At 11.00 hours Sgt. N. N. Mirsky reported to me that the prisoner has considerably improved and that he is sitting on his bunk instead of continuously sleeping as on the previous day.

Saw prisoner together with Interpreter Dubchin-skaya at 13.50 hours and asked him how he felt. On our entry he rose from his bunk and stood to attention. He replied that he felt fine and thanked me for the treatment which he had received. I told him that if he needed anything I would try to help him, to which he replied: "Thank you."

Though in much better shape than the previous day, the prisoner appears still very weak. His cheeks and eyes are hollow and it is notable that he has lost a considerable amount of weight. But he stubbornly tries to give the impression that he is fit.

At 18.04 hours Dr. Richter reported to me that the prisoner responds well to the diet, that he is regaining strength, but that the treatment should be continued for another two to three days, to get the man fully back on his feet again.

Telephoned Investigation Judge Col. I. S. Zhabotin at 18.30 hours and submitted report on prisoner. Col. Zhabotin sanctioned continuation of doctor's treatment and requested me to report to him further progress on the prisoner on 7.5.1956 at 10.30 hours.

Signed: Lt.-Col. G. G. Zuskin.

Report read: Col. I. S. Zhabotin.

REPORT FROM LIEUTENANT-COLONEL G. G. ZUSKIN

Sunday, May 6, 1956. 19.10 hours.

Dr. K. B. Richter reported to me at 10.00 and 18.30 hours further improvement of the prisoner's condition, advising that treatment should continue.

Sgt. O. P. Eykhler reported at 16.00 hours, having taken over duty, that the prisoner sits almost continuously on his bunk, staring in front of him. He eats his food obediently.

Signed: Lt.-Col. G. G. Zuskin.

Report read: Col. I. S. Zhabotin.

REPORT FROM LIEUTENANT-COLONEL G. G. ZUSKIN

Monday, May 7, 1956. 20.00 hours.

At 10.05 hours Medical Officer Dr. K. B. Richter

reported to me further progress of prisoner's recovery and stated that he will be fit enough to be put back on the bread and water diet and to physical exercises from tomorrow onwards.

Telephoned Investigation Judge Col. I. S. Zhabotin at 10.30 hours, informed him about Medical Officer's report, and received his order to comply with any request which the Interrogation Officer, who will be coming to see the prisoner tomorrow morning, might make.

Informed Sgt. O. P. Eykhler to be ready to recommence prisoner's physical exercises at short notice from tomorrow onward.

Signed: Lt.-Col. G. G. Zuskin.

Report read: Col. I. S. Zhabotin.

REPORT FROM CAPTAIN K. F. NIKOLAYEV

Tuesday, May 8, 1956. 09.00 hours.

Prisoner was brought to me in interrogation cell at 07.02 hours. Looked very pale and hollow-cheeked but appeared quite recovered and firm.

TRANSCRIPT FROM TAPE-BAND—OFFICIAL
TRANSLATION FROM ENGLISH

Capt. Nikolayev: "Have you now recovered from your illness, Commander?"
Crabb: "Yes, thank you."

Capt. Nikolayev: "And what have you decided to do? Are you ready to be sensible or are you still determined to continue as you have done up till now?"

Crabb: "I am determined to speak the truth."

Capt. Nikolayev: "Will you now admit that you attempted to carry out your underwater examination of the cruiser *Ordzhonikidze* for United States Naval Intelligence?"

Crabb: "I can't admit to something which is not true."

Capt. Nikolayev: "Will you admit now that the mysterious Mr. Smith is a high Naval Officer who followed you to Portsmouth to receive from you your first-hand report of your discoveries on the cruiser *Ordzhonikidze,* before you submitted your report to United States Naval Intelligence?"

Crabb: "I can't admit that, it is not true."

Capt. Nikolayev: "Do you admit that you carried out underwater examinations of the cruiser *Sverdlov* when she was on a friendly visit to England and lay at anchor at Portsmouth?"

Crabb: "I've already admitted it."

Capt. Nikolayev: "Do you admit now that you swam out to the cruiser *Sverdlov* on orders from United States Naval Intelligence?"

Crabb: "No, I did not. I searched the hull of the cruiser for an underwater time-bomb, which had been reported to have been placed there by anti-Russian refugees."

Capt. Nikolayev (voice raised): "I know this story.

But I want to hear the truth from you. So what is the truth?"

Crabb: "What I just told you."

Capt. Nikolayev: "So you are still determined to dish out packs of lies instead of speaking the truth."

Crabb: "I am speaking the truth."

Capt. Nikolayev: "And you still insist that you left the Sallyport Hotel together with your mysterious Matthew or Bernard Smith, that you went with him to the harbour, changed into your frogman's suit and went to carry out your underwater expedition merely out of personal curiosity?"

Crabb: "Yes."

Capt. Nikolayev: "If you think I will swallow this fable, you under-rate my intelligence, Commander."

Crabb: "I do not think anything, I merely tell you the truth."

Capt. Nikolayev: "In other words, in every detail you still stick to your version which you have told us on several occasions?"

Crabb: "Yes. I stick to the truth."

Capt. Nikolayev: "All right then. If you won't accept a helping hand, you'll have only yourself to blame if fate is not so kind to you. That is all. I'll have you taken back to your cell."

(END OF THE TRANSCRIPT OF THE TAPE-RECORDING.)

Had prisoner escorted back to his cell and went to see Prison Commandant Lt.-Col. G. G. Zuskin. Informed him of prisoner's stubbornness and requested him to make immediate arrangements for full physical training and bread and water punishment to be resumed.

Signed: Capt. K. F. Nikolayev.

Report read: Col. I. S. Zhabotin.

REPORT FROM LIEUTENANT-COLONEL G. G. ZUSKIN

Tuesday, May 8, 1956, 20.30 hours

Capt. K. F. Nikolayev saw me at 08.25 hours and informed me of the persistent stubbornness which the prisoner still maintains. He suggested that bread and water punishment and full physical training should be resumed without delay. I agreed, and gave immediate orders to this effect.

Sgt. O. P. Eykhler reported to me at 20.10 hours that he subjected the prisoner to hard physical training from 08.45 to 09.45, from 12.15 to 13.15, from 15.45 to 16.45 and from 19.00 to 20.00 hours. The prisoner complied to all commands without murmur but his movements are notably slower and less exact from exercise to exercise and there are clear signs of progressive exhaustion. Ordered Sgt. Eykhler to leave out the fifth exercise tonight, but to commence tomorrow full physical exercises.

Corporal Yavor reported at 20.23 hours that the prisoner eats his black bread in small quantities, and drinks very little. Each time he is escorted back to his cell from the prison yard, he at once falls on his bunk and is asleep immediately.

Signed: Lt.-Col. G. G. Zuskin.

Report read: Col. I. S. Zhabotin.

REPORT FROM LIEUTENANT-COLONEL G. G. ZUSKIN

Wednesday, May 9, 1956. 22.15 hours

At 21.44 hours Sgt. O. P. Eykhler reported to me that he subjected the prisoner to hard physical training from 06.30 to 07.30, from 10.00 to 11.00, from 13.30 to 14.30, from 17.00 to 18.00 and from 20.30 to 21.30 hours. Prisoner is rapidly losing his physical strength but, when on various occasions Sgt. Eykhler asked him through Interpreter Dubchinskaya whether he wanted to rest, he did not avail himself of the offers, but carried on, though his movements were slower and slower and less and less exact. Sgt. Eykhler expressed his renewed admiration of the prisoner's will-power and repeated his doubts as to whether his spirit can be broken.

Sgt. N. N. Mirsky reported to me at 21.59 hours that the prisoner hardly eats or drinks anything, although today he was given fresh bread and water. During the times between the physical exercises he lies on his bunk and sleeps heavily. Each time he was called for his physical exercises, Sgt. Mirsky had to shake him hard to wake him up. Not once did he protest or utter a single word, and obediently left his cell to be handed over to Sgt. Eykhler. Sgt. Mirsky expresses the opinion that the prisoner will soon collapse, but despite his report I did not think it necessary to call Medical Officer Dr. K. B. Richter, or to relax the prisoner's treatment.

Signed: Lt.-Col. G. G. Zuskin.

Report read: Col. I. S. Zhabotin.

REPORT FROM LIEUTENANT-COLONEL G. G. ZUSKIN

Thursday, May 10, 1956. 22.55 hours

Sgt. O. P. Eykhler reported to me at 21.40 hours that he subjected the prisoner to hard physical training from 06.30 to 07.30, from 10.00 to 11.00, from 13.30 to 14.30, from 17.00 to 18.00 and 20.30 to 21.30 hours. The prisoner is in worse shape than yesterday. He complies with all commands given but his movements are very shaky and not exact. At 17.48 hours he fell and seemed to be unable to get up. Through Interpreter Dubchinskaya, Sgt. Eykhler offered to cut short prisoner's training. But the prisoner, who had gradually managed to get on his feet again, refused, thanking Sgt. Eykhler for his offer. At the last exercise the prisoner compiied with Sgt. Eykhler's orders, clearly only with most determined will-power, but his movements were most inaccurate and shaky. Prisoner did not collapse again, but Sgt. Eykhler expects this to happen at any moment.

Sgt. N. N. Mirsky reported to me at 22.02 hours that throughout the day prisoner hardly ate or drank, and that during the times he is in his cell he sleeps heavily on his bunk. Judging from his observations of the prisoner, Sgt. Mirsky expects him to collapse at any time.

On account of these reports I thought it justifiable to call in Medical Officer Dr. K. B. Richter. With him and with Interpreter Dubchinskaya, I went to prisoner's cell at 22.25 hours. Prisoner was in a deep sleep and had to be shaken hard to be woken up. When Dr. Richter had finished his examinations, the prisoner thanked him but added that his efforts were only a waste of time as it is obvious that he is slowly to be killed off. Instead of Dr. Richter, I replied that no such thing is intended, but prisoner merely forced a smile to his face and muttered: "Thank you, anyway."

Dr. Richter found prisoner's physical condition to be very low and says that sooner or later he is bound to collapse. To my question whether the continued punishment treatment might kill the man, the Medical Officer replied that there is no such danger provided we don't go too far.

Telephoned Investigation Judge Col. I. S. Zhabotin at 22.40 hours but was told he was not on duty. Spoke to Major T. A. Dubnikov and reported to him on the prisoner. Major Dubnikov suggested that no change should be introduced. I gave the necessary orders.

Signed: Lt.-Col. G. G. Zuskin.

Report read: Col. I. S. Zhabotin.

REPORT FROM LIEUTENANT-COLONEL G. G. ZUSKIN

Friday, May 11, 1956. 16.30 hours.

At 14.06 hours Sgt. O. P. Eykhler reported to me that the prisoner had collapsed at 13.59 hours and had been unable to get up again. As he was satisfied that the prisoner was only semi-conscious, on his own responsibility he ordered that the prisoner be carried to his cell. Sgt. Eykhler stated that during the physical training from 06.30 to 07.30 hours the prisoner clearly showed great determination and will-power to comply with every command. But he was very shaky and Sgt. Eykhler was surprised that he did not collapse. During the physical training between 10.00 and 11.00 hours, the prisoner fell at 10.33 hours, but managed to get up again. At 10.56 hours he again fell and found it very difficult to regain his feet. Due to the prisoner's physical condition, Sgt. Eykhler cut short the physical training by four minutes. When brought to the prison yard again at 13.30 hours, the prisoner walked very unsteadily but complied silently with Sgt. Eykhler's commands. Fell at 13.42 hours but managed to get to his feet after 20 seconds. Collapsed finally at 13.59 hours.

Spoke to Medical Officer Dr. K. B. Richter at 14.15 hours and went with him to prisoner's cell. Dr. Richter states that prisoner is now in a state of complete exhaustion and if the present treatment continues, rapid deterioration will result.

Telephoned investigation judge, Col. I. S. Zhabotin, at 14.36 hours and reported the prisoner's state to him. Col. Zhabotin ordered me to send the man to him at the Naval Intelligence Station as soon as the medical officer's report states that he is fit to be transported.

At 16.05 hours Dr. Richter stated that prisoner has recovered. Ordered Sgt. N. N. Mirsky to escort prisoner in prison van to Khimky Naval Intelligence Station and informed Investigation Judge Col. I. S. Zhabotin that prisoner had left at 16.22 hours.

Signed: Lt.-Col. G. G. Zuskin.

Report read: Col. I. S. Zhabotin.

TRANSCRIPT FROM TAPE-BAND RECORDED FROM INTER-
ROGATION ROOM ON FRIDAY, MAY 11, 1956, 17.08
HOURS. RECORDED IN ENGLISH, OFFICIAL TRANSLATION.
INVESTIGATION JUDGE IVAN SEMYONOVICH ZHABOTIN
INTERROGATED   PRISONER—ENGLISH   NAVAL   COM-
MANDER LIONEL CRABB

Col. Zhabotin: "You don't look at all well, Commander. Is there anything I could do for you?"

Crabb: "No thanks. I am all right."

Col. Zhabotin: "Look here, your pride won't get
you far—it won't get you anywhere. I want to help
you, if you will let me, but I want at least some
co-operation from you."

Crabb (firm voice): "I'm afraid you're barking up
the wrong tree. I will never sign a false confession to
save my bacon."

Col. Zhabotin: "Who asks you for a confession? I
did not even ask you to make a statement. All I asked
was for you to help me to check the information I
have." (16 seconds' silence. Col. Zhabotin continues):
"Why should I need your confession or statement?
You have not co-operated with me, but this did not
stop the Soviet Government from lodging a Protest
Note with the British Government on the 4th of
May about a frogman having been seen on the 19th
of April near our Soviet ships." (9 seconds' silence.
Col. Zhabotin continues): "It may interest you to
know that two days ago, on the 9th of May, your
Prime Minister, Anthony Eden, sent a Diplomatic
Note to the Soviet Ambassador in London,
acknowledging that you, Commander Crabb, were
apparently carrying out frogman exercises, and

adding: 'Her Majesty's Government expresses regret for this incident.' And on the same day he told the House of Commons that it would not be in the public interest to disclose the circumstances of your death, and added: 'What was done was without the authority or knowledge of Ministers.' You see, Commander Crabb, that we are not lost, that we don't depend on your co-operation at all." (7 seconds' silence. Col. Zhabotin continues): "Have a Papiros, Commander."

Crabb: "Thank you."

Col. Zhabotin: "If you will only understand that I am not interested in hearing secrets from you, you will make life much easier for yourself. You can take it for granted that we do not need *you* for finding out valuable secrets. For this sort of thing we have specialists who know their job—people like those who informed us about your doings on the 19th of April and so helped us to grab you. What I want from you is your co-operation so that I can put together some insignificant missing links in the chain. And that is, I am sure, really a modest request."

Crabb: "What do you want to know?"

Col. Zhabotin: "Nothing—at the moment. I am no longer even interested in whether you confirm that you examined the *Ordzhonikidze's* hull for American Naval Intelligence or not. You see, Commander, even if you volunteered to sign a statement to the effect that you spied for the Yanks, it would be of no value to us. You are officially dead, and it is not opportune for us to destroy this myth, because we do not wish to make it known that we captured you and took you with us. So, perhaps you understand now that admissions or denials from you are no longer of interest to us."

Crabb (sounding puzzled): "I must admit that I do not follow what you are driving at. First you are annoyed when I don't confirm your story, then you do everything in your power to break me down, and suddenly you get me here and tell me all this."

Col. Zhabotin: "Conditions change sometimes, my friend. But don't let that worry you for the moment. Concentrate now on your recovery. Next time I see you, I hope to meet the Commander Buster Crabb as he was when he entered the water in Portsmouth on the 19th of April."

END OF TRANSCRIPT FROM TAPE-BAND.

REPORT FROM SERGEANT N. N. MIRSKY
Friday, May 11, 1956. 19.00 hours.

Took charge of prisoner at 16.15 hours, handcuffed him and escorted him to prison van. Left Lefortovo Prison at 16.22 hours and handed prisoner over at 16.59 hours to duty officer at Khimky Naval Intelligence Station. Duty officer ordered me and van to wait and to take prisoner back when ready.

At 17.48 hours duty officer handed prisoner back to me and ordered me to proceed direct to Lefortovo Prison. Handcuffed the prisoner and escorted him back to the prison van. Left Khimky Naval Intelligence Station at 17.54 hours and arrived at Lefortovo Prison at 18.49 hours.

Signed: Sgt. N. N. Mirsky.
Report read: Col. I. S. Zhabotin.

REPORT FROM LIEUTENANT-COLONEL G. G. ZUSKIN
Friday, May 11, 1956. 19.40 hours.

Received telephonic orders from Investigation Judge Col. I. S. Zhabotin at 17.45 hours to cancel prisoner's present punishment and to make immediate preparations for "favoured prisoner treatment", including prison officer food, in order to gain his confidence. Instructed all officers accordingly.

Saw prisoner in his cell at 19.15 hours together with Interpreter Dubchinskaya. Informed him that his strict routine was now suspended. But in order to dispel any possible suspicion of the true reason for the sudden change, I added that this was to continue only as long as he does not cause trouble. He looked straight in my eyes, thanked me, and said that he has no intention of causing trouble, whatever happens.

Signed: Lt.-Col. G. G. Zuskin.
Report read: Col. I. S. Zhabotin.

REPORT FROM LIEUTENANT-COLONEL G. G. ZUSKIN
Saturday, May 12, 1956. 17.30 hours.

Sgt. N. N. Mirsky reported to me at 15.00 hours that the prisoner hungrily eats all his food and already shows signs of general improvement. When Sgt. Mirsky, with the help of Interpreter Dubchinskaya, asked him after breakfast whether he would care to join the prison team in a game of football in the afternoon, the prisoner did not remain silent, as in the past, but replied that he would like to. He also accepted Sgt. Mirsky's Papiros and smoked it eagerly.

Sgt. O. P. Eykhler reported to me at 16.45 hours

that the prisoner played football with the prison team on the prison playground. He appeared very pleased and seemed to be his former self for the first time since his arrival.

Saw prisoner at 17.10 hours and was surprised to see how much he has already improved. He appears quite lively. He again thanked me for the interest I took in him and said that he appreciates what I did for him. For tactical reasons I did not tell him that it was the investigation judge, Col. I. S. Zhabotin, who was responsible for the change.

Signed: Lt.-Col. G. G. Zuskin.

Report read: Col. I. S. Zhabotin.

(Lieutenant-Colonel G. G. Zuskin's daily reports from May 13 to May 21 divulge that Commander Crabb was no longer interrogated, that he received sufficient prison officer's food, and that he was allowed to play football and baseball with favoured prisoners and guards in the grounds of Lefortovo Prison. These reports are not reproduced here because they are very much on the lines of Lieut.-Col. Zuskin's previous report.)

REPORT FROM LIEUTENANT-COLONEL G. G. ZUSKIN

Tuesday, May 22, 1956. 10.30 hours.

Investigation Judge Colonel I. S. Zhabotin telephoned me at 10.08 hours and requested me to send the prisoner to Khimky. He also told me he is leaving Moscow and that Investigation Judge Col. Aleksei Feofilovich Myaskov will be in charge of the case from now onward. Col. Zhabotin requested me to inform the prisoner and to impress upon him that Col. Myaskov does not allow any disobedience.

Informed prisoner accordingly and handed him over at 10.21 hours to Sgt. O. P. Eykhler for transport to the Naval Intelligence Station in Khimky. Prisoner left at 10.27 hours for Khimky.

Signed: Lt.-Col. G. G. Zuskin.

Report read: Col. A. F. Myaskov.

TRANSCRIPT FROM TAPE-BAND, RECORDED FROM INTER-ROGATION ROOM ON TUESDAY, MAY 22, 1956, 11.21 HOURS. RECORDED IN ENGLISH, OFFICIAL TRANSLATION. INVESTIGATION JUDGE ALEKSEI FEOFILOVICH MYASKOV INTERROGATES PRISONER—ENGLISH NAVAL COM-MANDER LIONEL CRABB

Col. Myaskov: "What have you decided to do, Crabb? Are you prepared to answer my questions or are you still stubborn?"

Crabb: "What do you want to know?"

Col. Myaskov: "Tell me what you discovered when you examined the *Ordzhonikidze* hull."

Crabb: "Nothing. As soon as I approached the cruiser and applied my measuring instrument, I heard the alarm device. Realising that the game was up, I did my best to get away."

Col. Myaskov: "So you found out that we don't take chances, eh?"

Crabb: "I did."

Col. Myaskov: "Why didn't you throw your

incriminating measuring instrument away while swimming to safety?"

Crabb: "What good would it have done? If I was caught it was irrelevant whether I had the instrument or not."

Col. Myaskov: "You have vast experience as a Naval frogman?"

Crabb: "I have."

Col. Myaskov: "And you can carry out almost any underwater job?"

Crabb: "I think so."

Col. Myaskov: "Suppose you had not been caught and were still in Portsmouth, and the Navy would ask you to undertake another underwater examination of a Soviet vessel, would you refuse to do it?"

Crabb: "I don't think so. But I suppose next time I would be more careful."

Col. Myaskov: "In other words, you do not regret what you did?"

Crabb: "I regret that I was caught."

Col. Myaskov: "You realise, of course, that what you say amounts to an admission of spying?"

Crabb: "I do. But it is not in my code of honesty to deny what I did."

Col. Myaskov: "You are a strange man, Crabb. You don't even try to dish up a story that all you did was an innocent morning swim."

Crabb: "I don't believe in lies."

Col. Myaskov: "You know, of course, that we can shoot you for spying?"

Crabb: "I do."

Col. Myaskov: "Would you consider buying your

life by giving us information about Allied Naval
secrets?"

Crabb: "I would not. I am not a traitor to my
country."

Col. Myaskov: "Yet, your country betrayed you.
Your country declared you dead without having
made the slightest move to ascertain whether this is
so or not. But let's not elaborate on this theme. You
don't want to agree to give us information on Allied
Naval secrets. But don't be surprised when I tell you
that all you know we know, too. We know probably
much more than you do. We have excellent men
everywhere."

Crabb: "What do you need *me* for then?"

(Noise as if table hit with fist.)

Col. Myaskov (raised voice): "You know that some
almost perfect reports need clarification in one way
or another. And you are the man who could help us
with it. This is why we did not drown you on the spot
but brought you to Moscow instead."

Crabb: "I'm afraid I cannot help you."

Col. Myaskov (raised voice): "You damned silly
English fool. Don't you realise that once we have
pressed all your knowledge out of you we can do away
with you?"

(4¼ seconds' silence.)

Crabb: "Why haven't you done it already?"

Col. Myaskov: "Because we did not want to
destroy your brain. We may have further use for you.
But if you continue your damned silly nonsense, we
will do what I said. I ask you now for the last time:
will you do as I ask you or not?"

Crabb: "I will not. Drug me if you wish. Shoot me if you wish. But you can't persuade me to betray my country."

(Noise of chair being pushed aside. Steps. Opening and shutting of door. Except prisoner's breathing, silence for 19.55 minutes. Opening and shutting of door. Steps. Noise of chair being pushed.)

Col. Myaskov: "You know, Crabb, I admire your British spirit. Have a Papiros."

(9 seconds' pause. Noise of striking match.)

Crabb: "Thank you."

Col. Myaskov: "You have at least proved that you are loyal to your country, if nothing else. This does not, of course, erase the crime you committed against our country, where this is the most serious crime which can be committed." ($7\frac{1}{2}$ seconds' silence. Col. Myaskov continues): "I must, however, tell you that we do not like to rub out people who are valuable in one way or another—that is, if we can help it. And you, Crabb, with your vast experience as a Naval frogman, are doubtless of certain value." (8 seconds' silence. Col. Myaskov continues): "I am therefore giving you the chance to join the Red Navy as a frog-man instead of passing you on to the Military Tribunal for sentence. You would be paid according to scale, which in your case would be the equivalent of about a thousand pounds a year. What have you to say to this?"

(76 seconds only heavy breathing.)

Crabb: "Provided I agree, would that mean that you would order me to make underwater surveys of British or other Allied vessels?"

Col. Myaskov (voice raised, sounding annoyed):
"Look here, Crabb, I am giving you a chance to save
your life and earning your living honestly by following your profession, and you start to make conditions.
You are not in a position to make conditions. You
either accept what I am offering you or take the consequences. So what is your answer?"

Crabb: "I can only answer if I know what my
duties will be."

Col. Myaskov (voice raised): "Your duties will be
what they will be. How can I know what your commanding officer will order you to do?" ($5\frac{3}{4}$ seconds'
silence. Col. Myaskov continues): "We can make use
of you, but we can also do without you. But I tell you
here and now: if you decide to remain unco-operative
we will not feed you to keep you as a museum piece.
We will rub you out." (69 seconds' silence. Col.
Myaskov, low, penetrating voice): "You know,
Crabb, that as far as your own authorities are concerned, you are dead. In order to prove their theory,
we are quite willing to let them find your body—or,
to make it quite clear to you, a body which would be
accepted as yours. When this is found, the dead Naval
Commander Lionel Crabb could be buried in
England while the live Crabb could work undetected
and unsuspected in our Navy."

(Noise of a chair being pushed aside. Steps. Opening of door.)

Col. Myaskov: "Bring the stretcher in."

(Steps. Noise of putting something down. Steps.
Shutting of door.)

Col. Myaskov: "Now let's see what's under the

rubber sheet." (18 seconds' pause, some rustling. Col. Myaskov continues): "This one should fit your description. Don't you agree, Crabb?"

Crabb: "I'm afraid I don't. Looking at this dead man, I cannot see the slightest resemblance to me."

Col. Myaskov: "The body measurements are near enough the same as yours and that's all that matters. As an experienced Naval frogman you ought to know that if a body is left in the sea long enough, it decomposes to such an extent that not even the best experts can recognise it, or even establish the cause of death. But in order to enable your people to establish your identity, the body would naturally have everything you wore when you went out for your spying attempt of the *Ordzhonikidze's* hull."

(Noise of chair being pushed aside. Steps. Opening of door.)

Col. Myaskov: "You can remove the body now."

(Steps. Shutting of door. Steps. Noise of chair being pushed about.)

Col. Myaskov: "You see now that I not only mean to give you the chance to join our Navy, but that I am even prepared to do everything in my power to help your authorities to establish your death without doubt. But don't think that you can continue to play cat and mouse with me any longer. If in your stupidity you still refuse my offer, you won't leave this station alive. And if this should be the case, your real body will be washed up somewhere near Portsmouth." (46 seconds' silence. Col. Myaskov continues): "What is your answer now, Crabb?"

(35 seconds' silence.)

Crabb: "Under the circumstances, I accept."

Col. Myaskov: "I knew that even you, Crabb, have your price. Your final decision does not come as a surprise to me. But I must warn you to give up any hopes of double-crossing us. You can take it from me that there is no escape from us. On the other hand, if you work honestly and to the best of your abilities, you will be treated like any other member of the Soviet Navy. We appreciate good work and initiative, and those who distinguish themselves are honoured to the full."

END OF TRANSCRIPT FROM TAPE-BAND.

REPORT FROM SECOND LIEUTENANT V. A. CHERTOK
Tuesday, May 22, 1956. 17.00 hours

At 13.12 hours Investigation Judge Col. A. F. Myaskov ordered me to take the prisoner to the rehabilitation centre of the State Security Commission in Selskoye, and handed the Englishman over to me. I handcuffed the man and led him to the prison van. Managed to tell him in my broken English not to cause any trouble as it would be useless. The Englishman replied that he had no such intentions.

During the journey, when we had been on our way for over an hour, the Englishman asked me where he was being taken. I replied "dunno", having no instructions as to whether to tell him or not. The Englishman did not make further attempts to find out, but accepted the Papirosi which I offered him and which he smoked eagerly.

At 15.19 hours, arrived at the Selskoye centre and escorted the Englishman direct to the reception office, where I handed him over to the duty officer, Lieutenant Baidukov.

Returned to base at 16.55 hours.

Signed: Second Lieutenant V. A. Chertok.

Report read: Col. A. F. Myaskov.

REPORT FROM LIEUTENANT K. U. BAIDUKOV
Tuesday, May 22, 19.30 hours.

At 13.38 hours Commandant Major Klim Osipovich Krasenko informed me over the intercom telephone to expect in under two hours an Englishman who had left Khimky Naval Intelligence Station at 13.15 hours and was on his way to our centre. He also told me that Sgt. Vira Nikolayevna Savelyeva had been assigned as an interpreter and that she is to be available at any time I may require her services for speaking to the Englishman.

Second Lieutenant Chertok handed over the English prisoner from Khimky Naval Intelligence Station. I asked the prisoner in Russian to take a seat. But the prisoner clearly did not understand what I said and explained in English: "I do not understand Russian." But this I could not understand. I summoned Woman Sergeant Vira Nikolayevna Savelyeva, who arrived at once. Through her I told him that he is going to spend some time at this rehabilitation centre—provided the commandant does not decide otherwise. As Commandant Major Klim Osipovich Krasenko was not yet ready to see the prisoner, I asked Sergeant Savelyeva to take the Englishman to the eating room to get him a meal. On returning to the reception office at 17.42 hours, Sgt. Savelyeva

reported that the only words which were spoken
between her and the Englishman were whether he
had had enough to eat or whether he wanted more.
At 20.37 hours Commandant Major Klim Osipovich
Krasenko ordered me by the intercom telephone, to
send the Englishman up to him. Sgt. Savelyeva
escorted the man to the commandant's office.

Signed: Lieutenant K. U. Baidukov.

Report read: Col. A. F. Myaskov.

REPORT FROM MAJOR KLIM OSIPOVICH KRASENKO, COM-
MANDANT OF THE STATE SECURITY COMMISSION'S
REHABILITATION CENTRE AT SELSKOYE

Tuesday, May 22, 21.20 hours.

At 13.20 hours Investigation Judge Colonel A. F.
Myaskov telephoned me and informed me that at
13.15 hours he had sent a special prisoner, the English
Naval Commander Crabb to the centre, to have him
observed as to reliability before making final
decisions as to whether he is suitable for enlistment
in the Red Navy, and also to teach him the Russian
language as thoroughly as possible. Made immediate
arrangements for the reception of the Englishman,
detailed Sgt. Vira Nikolayevna Savelyeva, who knows
English, as Crabb's Russian teacher, and informed
reception office duty officer, Lieutenant K. U.
Baidukov, to expect the Englishman.

At 20.43 Sgt. Savelyeva escorted the English Commander to my interrogation office on the second floor,
in which the recording machine was switched on.
Though my English is imperfect, I preferred to speak
to the commander alone, and dismissed Sgt. Savelyeva.

TRANSCRIPT FROM TAPE-BAND, RECORDED FROM INTER-
ROGATION OFFICE ON TUESDAY, MAY 22, 1956, 20.46
HOURS. RECORDED IN ENGLISH, OFFICIAL TRANSLATION.
COMMANDANT MAJOR KLIM OSIPOVICH KRASENKO TO
ENGLISH NAVAL COMMANDER LIONEL CRABB

Maj. Krasenko: "I know all about you. There is
therefore no need for you to tell me anything. You
have been brought here to acclimatise yourself to
Soviet life. The first thing you will do is to learn
Russian. You must work hard so that you do not
waste precious time. I will study your daily progress
reports. Your life has now been completely changed
for you. Therefore you will forget who you are. For
the next ten years you have enlisted in the Red Navy
and from now on you will be known as Lev Lvovich
Korablov. Your salary will be according to scale from
the day you take up your duties. And if you prove
yourself reliable you may be allowed to go wherever
you want, after your ten years' service is at an end."

($2\frac{1}{2}$ seconds' silence.)

Maj. Krasenko: "I must add that all that has been
said naturally applies only if your record is clean in
every respect. I want you to be clear about this, and
that as long as you are in the Red Navy, either in the
Soviet Union or in some other territorial waters,
there will never be a chance for you to double-cross
us or try to escape from us. You will be watched day
and night, and let it be said that, at the first wrong
step you take, you will be shot and there will be no
second chance."

(4 seconds' silence.)

Maj. Krasenko: "Investigation Judge Colonel Myaskov is fully aware of the fact that he is not only taking a very great risk but also tremendous responsibility in giving you the possibility of joining the Red Navy, instead of having you shot as a despicable spy. With many saboteurs and wreckers Colonel Myaskov has the reputation of being one of the most ruthless investigating judges of the State Security Commission, but you, Commander Crabb, or, to call you by your new name, Lev Lvovich Korablov, have discovered by your own experience that he is a very fair man and always ready to give a prisoner a chance. But don't think he is a man who would ever forgive anyone who made the slightest attempt to trespass on his generosity. Anyone who takes the slightest step in the wrong direction finds out that Colonel Myaskov can also be completely merciless. So, always remember my well-meant words of today, and if you behave as is expected of any other law-abiding citizen, and if you work to the best of your abilities, then, Lev Lvovich Korablov, you will soon find that you have made the right decision and that you have chosen the finest career in the world."

END OF TAPE-RECORDING TRANSCRIPT.

I did not ask for an answer or comment and Korablov did not say anything.

Called Sergeant Savelyeva and ordered her to take Korablov to barrack y11.

Signed: Maj. K. O. Krasenko.

Report read: Col. A. F. Myaskov.

REPORT FROM SERGEANT VIRA NIKOLAYEVNA SAVELYEVA

Tuesday, May 22, 1956. 22.00 hours.

Commandant Major K. O. Krasenko ordered me at 20.59 hours to escort L. L. Korablov to barrack y11.

On the way I told him that he was to share his room with three others, but that for the time being he would be unable to speak to them as they were Russians and do not know English. On arriving in his room he did not say anything about the room being furnished only with four bunks, a bench and a table, but answered my remark that I hoped he will be happy here with: "I surely will. It is much better than my previous accommodation."

I then told him:

"I am now your Russian teacher. You must listen to what I tell you. You must work hard. Here in the Soviet Union we work to plan. Your plan is to learn Russian very quickly. The tovarich commandant will be studying my reports about you. You must work hard or he will be a very furious major. I don't want that. He could be furious with me also. So you must learn very well."

L. L. Korablov said he was eager to learn Russian and I told him that the lessons will start tomorrow morning at 09.30 hours and will last till 18.30 hours, with one hour break for lunch.

Signed: Sgt. V. N. Savelyeva.

Report read: Col. A. F. Myaskov.

REPORT FROM MAJOR BORIS MARKOVICH SMIRNOV,
SPECIAL COMMISSION, STATE SECURITY COMMITTEE,
LENINGRAD

Monday, May 28, 1956. 16.00 hours.

Body is now ready for submersion in the sea. On
advice from medical experts, head and both hands
have been removed to exclude all possible identification. Medical experts say that the body must be submerged in the sea for at least 1½ years to decompose
to such an extent that no doctor in the world can
establish either the cause of death or any possible
identification marks.

The body, bearing all the clothes which the
prisoner wore when captured, including his
measuring instrument and the prisoner's frogman
suit, inclusive of flippers, has been submerged in the
sea since 15.10 hours. To obviate losing the body,
indestructible steel-wire has been carefully fixed on
its legs, so that it is now safely anchored in the sea.
To exclude unauthorised people accidentally discovering the body, I have ordered the area to be
fenced in.

Taking into consideration the medical experts'
opinion about the length of time it takes to decompose the body sufficiently for our needs, inspection
will not take place prior to 1¼ years; therefore, the
fencing will not be taken down too often. When the
body is inspected in August, 1957, I will submit my
detailed report about the state of the body.

Signed: Maj. Boris Markovich Smirnov.

Report read: Col. A. F. Myaskov.

(The *dossier* now contains daily progress reports from Sgt. V. N. Savelyeva up to June 20, 1956. They all confirm that Commander Crabb received daily eight solid hours of tuition in Russian, that, "due to the fact that he is eager to learn the language so as to be able to talk to the Russians," he has made remarkable progress. They also show that the commandant of Selskoye Rehabilitation Centre was pleased with the "willingness of L. L. Korablov" and that, in order to show him his appreciation, he no longer confined him to his barrack room, but permitted him to walk about on his own in the grounds of the establishment during his free time. The last of Sgt. Savelyeva's daily reports is, however, reproduced below, so as to acquaint the reader with how she worded her progress reports.)

REPORT FROM SERGEANT V. N. SAVELYEVA
Thursday, June 21, 1956. 19.00 hours.

Rating Korablov continues to be most eager to learn the Russian language as perfectly as possible, and his daily progress is remarkable. He is already now able to read *Pravda* and other newspapers, with the help of the dictionary, of course.

Today when I asked him to read the article which *Pravda* printed on May 30, about the decorations of Rear-Admiral Kotov and Captain Stiepanov, he managed to do it satisfactorily. But when I asked him quite harmlessly in the midst of a general conversation whether he could guess what the two commanders had done, he merely shrugged his shoulders and said that he had no idea.

He can also converse with his room mates and other inhabitants of the centre, though only in a limited vocabulary. His conduct continues to be exemplary.

Signed: Sgt. V. N. Savelyeva.

Report seen: Col. A. F. Myaskov.

REPORT FROM MAJOR KLIM OSIPOVICH KRASENKO, COMMANDANT OF THE STATE SECURITY COMMISSION'S REHABILITATION CENTRE AT SELSKOYE

Friday, June 22, 1956. 19.30 hours.

L. L. Korablov is making remarkable progress as far as the Russian language is concerned and is already able to engage in everyday conversation. His pronunciation is, however, still quite bad, but even in this respect he is improving, especially these last few days.

He appears to have completely accepted his assignment and seems quite happy. He does not, however, show interest in political schooling and when approached on the subject he insists that his knowledge of the Russian language is as yet too poor to enable him to be able to follow a course. He also refuses to speak about his past life and even in private conversations with some of the women officers over a glass of tea he insists that the past is once and for all at an end, and that he is merely concentrating on the future.

It is estimated that in another month he may know sufficient Russian to be transferred to the naval establishment. A further report will be forwarded in two weeks in order to enable you to form your opinion about your future orders.

Signed: Major K. O. Krasenko.

Report seen: Col. A. F. Myaskov.

(The *dossier* again contains Sgt. Savelyeva's daily progress reports up to July 1, 1956. But because they merely record that Commander Crabb "is making continuously steady progress, not only in his knowledge of Russian but also in his pronunciation, which is rapidly improving," they are not reproduced in full.)

REPORT FROM LIEUTENANT I. I. GORBENKO AND SGT. V. N. SAVELYEVA

Monday, July 2, 1956. 22.10 hours.

Took L. L. Korablov to Moscow, as directed by Commandant Major K. O. Krasenko. When told at 08.00 hours to get ready to leave the centre, L. L. Korablov inquired whether he was leaving for good. When told that he was being given a free day in appreciation of his good work and discipline, and would be sightseeing in Moscow, he openly expressed his gratitude.

During the car drive from Selskoye to Moscow, L. L. Korablov watched the landscape and the numerous blocks of flats and factories which were either completed or in the course of erection with interest, and admitted that he was astonished to see such great building activity. When we reached

Moscow, he frankly expressed surprise at the countless new buildings which had been erected after the
war, and the dense motor traffic, and also the variety
of goods which he noticed in the shop windows.

He appeared impressed when taken to the Lenin
Mausoleum in Red Square, but he did not say anything. On passing a church and seeing that it was not
closed, L. L. Korablov remarked that he had not
thought that Russians were allowed to visit churches.
He was, however, most impressed when we took him
to the reconstructed parts of Moscow and when he
saw the airy thoroughfares with their high modern
buildings. He did not conceal his amazement. It
seems that best of all he likes the new Gorky
Street.

He was equally impressed when we visited the
G.U.M. store, when he found out for himself that
large numbers of ordinary people not only buy
articles of bare necessity but luxuries like television
sets, radio receivers, electric irons, etc. He admitted
that he had been under the impression that these
things were only available in Russia to the better-paid
circles, and said that, having seen the type of people
who spent their money in the store, he now knows
that every section of the population shops in the
store.

He enjoyed food and drink in the Caucasian
Restaurant and expressed his liking for the friendly
service which the waiters gave. On several occasions
he said that his first outing into freedom was like a
lovely dream and that he expected to wake up at any
moment and find himself back in reality.

During the whole day, only Russian was spoken and L. L. Korablov is well able to converse freely, though sometimes he is at a loss for a word and has to think to find the right expression.

The excursion to Moscow was a clear step forward to his being convinced that the Soviet people are not only prosperous but also contented. This opinion is based on the fact that L. L. Korablov repeatedly said that the faces of the people which crowd the streets, shops and restaurants are cheerful and that they look full of life.

Signed: Lieut. I. I. Gorbenko.

Sgt. V. N. Savelyeva.

Report read: Col. A. F. Myaskov.

REPORT FROM MAJOR KLIM OSIPOVICH KRASENKO, COMMANDANT OF THE STATE SECURITY COMMISSION'S REHABILITATION CENTRE AT SELSKOYE

Tuesday, July 3, 1956. 20.30 hours.

Received at 18.50 hours the following message from Khimky Naval Intelligence Station:

"Try to discover the state of Korablov's mind in order to enable me to assess when he is ripe for transfer to Naval Command. Advise you to inform him of rumours which have circulated about him abroad, as this might induce him to say an unguarded word. —Col. A. F. Myaskov."

Accordingly, summoned L. L. Korablov to my interrogation office at 19.00 hours.

TRANSCRIPT FROM TAPE-BAND, RECORDED FROM INTER-
ROGATION OFFICE ON TUESDAY, JULY 3, 1956,
19.00 HOURS. COMMANDANT MAJOR KLIM OSIPOVICH
KRASENKO AND L. L. KORABLOV

Maj. Krasenko: "I called you to tell you that news
about your being in the Soviet Union has leaked out
abroad. Sailors of the Red Navy blabbed in Denmark
that you were captured on April 19 and taken out of
British waters on board the *Ordzhonikidze.*" ($3\frac{3}{4}$
seconds' silence.)

Korablov: "How did the British authorities react
to this?"

Maj. Krasenko: "Not at all. Neither a Diplomatic
Note nor any other request was lodged. It appears
that they stick to their announcement that you are
dead." (8 seconds' silence.)

Korablov: "Then there is nothing to talk about."

Maj. Krasenko: "Supposing that the British
Government at a later date decides to demand a full
investigation, and supposing that some of your
former colleagues were to recognise you when you
are in the Red Navy, what would your reaction
be?"

Korablov: "I am officially dead, am I not? I am
now Lev Lvovich Korablov."

Maj. Krasenko (sounding satisfied): "I am glad to
hear that you don't regret your decision to work in
the Red Navy."

Korablov: "It is not my habit to regret any
decision I make."

Maj. Krasenko: "Am I then to understand that

IVAN SEROV. Russia's Secret Police Chief, responsible for mass murders and deportations during and after the war, came to Britain to check on the safety precautions for the visit of Russian leaders. He also visited Portsmouth on 24 March, 1956, where he succeeded in establishing communications between Red spies and the Russian warships in Portsmouth harbour. The Soviet Secret *Dossier* confirms that he was successful and that, in fact, shore agent 02SD regularly submitted his reports to the Russian flagship.

Russian sailors on leave in Stockholm. It was in Stockholm, Copenhagen and other ports of the free world where individual Russian
sailors and officers confirmed on various occasions that a prisoner
was taken on board the *Ordzhonikidze* in Portsmouth harbour on
19 April, 1956.

if by a million-to-one chance someone should identify you as Commander Lionel Crabb you would not avail yourself of the chance to be returned to England?"

Korablov: "Exactly."

Maj. Krasenko (benevolently): "And how do you find your new way of life? Have you any complaints?"

Korablov: "None whatsoever. I am treated well and I appreciate everything."

Maj. Krasenko: "You can rest assured that we will keep to our side of the bargain and that we will do everything to provide the British authorities with proof that Commander Lionel Crabb died during his underwater examination of the *Ordzhonikidze's* hull on April 19."

(2¾ seconds' silence.)

Maj. Krasenko: "I am sure it will interest you to know that the body which Colonel Myaskov showed you and which resembles you admirably is now anchored in the sea so as to make it fully suitable for our purposes. When the body is ready to withstand any expert examination depends on the mechanical and animal process of the sea. And when it is to be taken to England will be governed by the opportune moment. But you see that all the preparations which Colonel Myaskov indicated to you are being made."

Korablov: "I never doubted that Colonel Myaskov meant what he said."

Maj. Krasenko: "What, in your opinion, would be the most suitable work for you to carry out in the Red Navy?"

Korablov: "Work of a frogman."

Maj. Krasenko: "You have vast experience as a frogman?"

Korablov: "I have."

Maj. Krasenko: "Would you say that you could carry out *any* underwater job?"

Korablov: "My commanding officers thought so."

Maj. Krasenko: "Drop your English modesty. We here say what we think without being considered boasters."

Korablov: "Very well then. I can undertake *any* underwater job."

Maj. Krasenko: "That's better. Perhaps you will have the possibility of doing it." ($3\frac{3}{4}$ seconds' silence. Maj. Krasenko continues): "There is yet one snag attached to it. What would happen should you carry out underwater work in a foreign port and were captured by Western guards and identified as Commander Lionel Crabb?"

Korablov: "I can't see how that could be possible. I was told during my interrogation that the Admiralty announced me as dead. This fact was repeated to me on various occasions. How could they then identify me as Commander Lionel Crabb if Commander Crabb is officially declared dead?"

Maj. Krasenko: "They could change their minds and could suddenly admit that their announcement was made on account of insufficient information at the time, if you confirm to your captors that you are in fact Commander Crabb."

Korablov: "I have accepted to be Lev Lvovich Korablov. I don't think I need add any more to that."

Maj. Krasenko: "Very well then. I believe that you indeed mean what you say, and I don't doubt that all the necessary steps will be taken without delay to establish that the news which circulated in England, Germany and other foreign countries about your having been taken out of British waters on the cruiser *Ordzhonikidze* and being held prisoner in the Soviet Union is inconsistent with the actual truth."

END OF TAPE-RECORDING TRANSCRIPT.

Having observed most carefully how L. L. Korablov reacted to every single word I said and the way he replied, I am satisfied that he did not put on a show, but really means what he says. I anticipate that this report and enclosed tape-band of the recording of the conversation between myself and L. L. Korablov will assist you in making your further dispositions.

Signed: Maj. K. O. Krasenko.

Report read: Col. A. F. Myaskov.

MEMORANDUM FROM INVESTIGATION JUDGE COLONEL ALEKSEI FEOFILOVICH MYASKOV TO THE CENTRAL COMMITTEE OF THE COMMUNIST PARTY OF THE U.S.S.R.

Khimky, July 4, 1956.

Due to the special circumstances of the case, I recommend that renewed campaigns should be launched confirming that the British Naval Commander Lionel Crabb was killed in Portsmouth on April 19, while attempting to spy on the cruiser *Ordzhonikidze*. The reason for my recommendation is that foreign newspapers continuously publish prominently placed articles about Commander Crabb being held prisoner in the Soviet Union. In my opinion, if announcements are made at mass-meetings and in the Soviet press on the theme that Commander Crabb is dead, that his body floated out to sea, and if any details about how he died are given, I am convinced that these important revelations must find their way into the British and other Western press and so help to establish that all the reports about Commander Crabb's imprisonment in the Soviet Union are untrue, and that he died while diving in Portsmouth Harbour.

MEMORANDUM FROM THE CENTRAL COMMITTEE OF THE COMMUNIST PARTY OF THE U.S.S.R. TO INVESTIGATION JUDGE COL. A. F. MYASKOV

Moscow, July 5, 1956.

Your suggestion is valuable, and as campaigns on Commander Crabb's death can indeed dispel the harmful revelations of the British, German and other press, instructions to party organisers have already been given.

It was also recommended to the trade union movement to make the same arrangements.

The press department has been requested to arrange publicity, but due to the fact that conspicuous reports in the leading Soviet press might cause suspicion abroad, it has been ruled that reports about these campaigns should be published only in some newspapers of the provincial press.

REPORT FROM MAJOR KLIM OSIPOVICH KRASENKO,
COMMANDANT OF THE STATE SECURITY COMMISSION'S
REHABILITATION CENTRE AT SELSKOYE
Monday, July 9, 1956.
At 18.45 hours summoned L. L. Korablov to my
interrogation office, and informed him that a "Crabb
is Dead" campaign has been launched all over the
U.S.S.R., and that countless party organisers made
known at compulsory meetings at factories and other
establishments, the text of which had been supplied
to them on the subject. I read out the text to him.

TRANSCRIPT FROM TAPE-BAND, RECORDED FROM INTER-
ROGATION OFFICE ON MONDAY, JULY 9, 1956,
18.49 HOURS. COMMANDANT MAJOR KLIM OSIPOVICH
KRASENKO AND L. L. KORABLOV

Maj. Krasenko: "This is what the Partorgs* said
and what was published in wall gazettes in factories
and other establishments, and also in some newspapers of the provincial press: The well-known
British Naval frogman, Commander Lionel Crabb,
also known as Buster Crabb, who for his daring wartime services was invested with the high British
award, the George Medal, attempted to examine the
hull of our cruiser *Ordzhonikidze* for American
Naval Intelligence, on April 19, while our Naval
Squadron which had taken Marshal Bulganin and
Comrade Khrushchev to England for a good-will
visit, lay at anchor in Stokes Bay, near Portsmouth
Harbour."
(1 second silence.)
* Party organisers.

142

Maj. Krasenko: "Though the experienced under-water spy went about with greatest skill, his despicable doings were nevertheless detected. As he was about to examine the bottom of the cruiser *Ordzhonikidze,* his own measuring apparatus betrayed him, setting in motion the ingenious alarm devices of the cruiser."

(1 second silence.)

Maj. Krasenko: "The frogman spy was, consequently unable to give his overlords the valuable information which they had ordered him to obtain. He was killed by the screw which was automatically set in motion by the alarm devices at the right moment."

($2\frac{1}{4}$ seconds' silence.)

Maj. Krasenko: "Did you understand what I read out to you?"

Korablov: "Yes."

Maj. Krasenko: "Have you any comment to make?"

Korablov: "No."

Maj. Krasenko: "I will read you what the Proforgs* said. Unfortunately the trade unions did not co-operate with the party as they should have done, and the Proforgs gave a different version to that of the Partorgs. Due to lack of co-operation, both versions appeared at the same time, in wall gazettes in factories and other establishments. It is unfortunate, yes, but I don't think that any real harm has been done."

($2\frac{3}{4}$ seconds' silence.)

* Trade union organisers.

Maj. Krasenko: "This is what the Proforgs said and what trade union wall gazettes published: The frogman's measuring apparatus was detected by the alarm devices when he approached the bottom of the cruiser *Ordzhonikidze*. These ingenious alarm devices automatically set in motion powerful magnets which pinned the frogman to the bottom of the cruiser. When the alarm was investigated, and the magnets switched off, the frogman was found to have been drowned. But as a dead body of a frogman did not concern our vessels but was a strictly British affair, no steps were taken to recover the dead frogman spy from the sea or to inform the British authorities, though Rear-Admiral Kotov formally complained to the British that a frogman had been sighted near our warships which were on a friendly visit to Britain."

($3\frac{1}{2}$ seconds' silence.)

Maj. Krasenko: "What do you say to this slip-up?"

Korablov: "What can I say?"

Maj. Krasenko: "As I said before, it won't harm. Besides, there is a great possibility that the trade union wall-gazettes will escape being noticed."

END OF TRANSCRIPT OF TAPE-BAND.

I was unable to find out what Korablov really thought. He gave the impression of being entirely disinterested in the matter, which might be taken as a sign that he is determined to remain Korablov with no connection or interest in Crabb.

Signed: Maj. K. O. Krasenko.

Report read: Col. A. F. Myaskov.

(The *dossier* contains daily progress reports from Sgt. Savelyeva up to August 16, 1956. They all speak of the "extraordinary improvement which L. L. Korablov continuously makes both as far as his knowledge of the Russian language is concerned, and also as to his pronunciation". The later reports say that "L. L. Korablov is able to speak better, and his accent is improving. He also writes, but he still makes great mistakes, both in grammar and spelling." The two reports from Maj. K. O. Krasenko, on July 23 and August 6, 1956, which are also contained in the *dossier*, merely state that "L. L. Korablov continues to make progress in his studies of the Russian language and is one of the best-disciplined occupants of the centre. He is liked by everyone, because of his wit and his strong inclination towards comradeship." The other report, speaking again of the progress and exemplary behaviour, also says that "it seems to be clear that L. L. Korablov is eager to join the Red Navy as he appears to be the type who hates to be unable to follow his own profession".)

REPORT FROM MAJOR KLIM KRASENKO, COMMANDANT OF THE STATE SECURITY COMMISSION'S REHABILITATION CENTRE AT SELSKOYE

Friday, August 17, 1956. 11.15 hours.

At 10.25 hours, Investigation Judge Col. A. F. Myaskov telephoned me, ordered me to send L. L. Korablov to the Naval Intelligence Station, and informed me that he would not return to the centre. Summoned Korablov to my office and saw him at

10.36 hours. Informed him that he was going to see Investigation Judge Col. Myaskov, and would not be returning to Selskoye.

At 10.51 hours L. L. Korablov, accompanied by Lieutenant I. I. Gorbenko, left by car for Khimky.

Signed: Major K. O. Krasenko.

Report read: Col. A. F. Myaskov.

REPORT FROM INVESTIGATION JUDGE COLONEL
ALEKSEI FEOFILOVICH MYASKOV

Friday, August 17. 14.00 hours.

Requested Commandant Major K. O. Krasenko at 10.25 hours to send over L. L. Korablov, who was brought to me to the interrogation room at 12.26 hours.

TRANSCRIPT FROM TAPE-BAND, RECORDED FROM INTER-
ROGATION ROOM ON FRIDAY, AUGUST 17, 1956, 12.26
HOURS. INVESTIGATION JUDGE COLONEL ALEKSEI
FEOFILOVICH MYASKOV AND L. L. KORABLOV

Col. Myaskov: "Your conduct sheet, Lev Lvovich Korablov, records that you have been making progress and that you understand and now speak sufficient Russian to be able to follow your occupation. As there is no point in wasting any more valuable time, I am now transferring you to the Naval Command, where they will grade you according to your qualifications."

($2\frac{1}{2}$ seconds' silence.)

Col. Myaskov: "I hope you realise that I am taking a personal risk in not having passed you on to the

military tribunal for sentence, but am instead giving
you a chance to follow your occupation. I trust that
you won't let me down and that you won't repay
my humanitarian deed with possible unforgivable
attempts to double-cross us in one way or another."

($3\frac{1}{4}$ seconds' silence.)

Col. Myaskov: "I can only go by the reports which
I have regularly received about you—unfortunately
I cannot read what is going on in your mind. But I
hope that I am not making a grave mistake by trust-
ing you and so helping you to live as a free man, with
the possibility of working honestly and to the best of
your abilities in your own profession."

(58 seconds' pause. Sound of walking about.)

Col. Myaskov: "To avoid any misunderstanding,
I must tell you again that though you will from now
on become a member of the Red Navy, you will
nevertheless have no chance of planning any
escapades or submitting misleading information
about underwater examinations which you may be
ordered to carry out. Every move you will make while
in the Red Navy will be skilfully watched, and any
wrong step which you may choose to take will be
punished without mercy."

($2\frac{3}{4}$ seconds' silence.)

Col. Myaskov: "But I hope that my words of warning are unnecessary and that, instead, you will work
to the best of your ability and avail yourself of the
possibilities of gradually climbing back to the position you held in the British Navy. In our country we
reward initiative and good work, and those who
deserve it can—in a comparatively short time—

become high-ranking officers." (2 seconds' silence. Col. Myaskov continues): "Have you decided to become a worthy member of the Red Navy and to work honestly and to the best of your abilities?"

Korablov: "I have."

Col. Myaskov: "Then all that remains is for you to fill in the application form to join the Red Navy and sign it in your name of Lev Lvovich Korablov."

(9.41 minutes' pause. Rustling of paper. Breathing.)

Col. Myaskov: "You will now be paid eight hundred roubles, to which you are entitled for the time of your studies. I am also allowing you to select a complete civilian outfit for yourself so that you will arrive at the Naval Training Command like any other recruit. You will feel better when you finally take off your dungarees—and with them you will strip off your unpleasant past." (2½ seconds' silence. Col. Myaskov continues): "And as the train for Leningrad does not leave for some hours, I am allowing you to go sightseeing in our wonderful capital."

END OF TRANSCRIPT OF TAPE-BAND.

Handed over L. L. Korablov to Captain L. B. Chuikov, to whom I had previously given all the necessary instructions.

Signed: Col. A. F. Myaskov.

REPORT FROM CAPTAIN L. B. CHUIKOV

Saturday, August 18, 1956.

Handed over to L. L. Korablov his 800 roubles, receipt for which is enclosed.

L. L. Korablov did not at any time give any cause for complaint.

Though he told me that he had once before been sightseeing in Moscow, he was none the less impressed once more when I drove him about the town and showed him the numerous new dwelling houses either built after the war or now in the course of construction. When I showed him a photograph of old Gorky Street while taking him along the new thoroughfare, he clearly expressed his admiration for this unique showpiece of modern reconstruction.

He was equally impressed when taken to the G.U.M. store, said that even on his previous visit to the store he had been most surprised to see so many things on sale and people able to buy what they wanted, and added that his visit of today was a confirmation for him that many things are on sale at all times, and the people able to buy what they wish. When selecting his clothes he wanted to choose the cheapest articles, making it clear that he did not want to run up a high bill, especially as this was not being paid by him. I had to persuade him to take articles of a better standard, but when he saw the final amount of his purchases, he offered to contribute with his own money to keep the amount down.

When I tried to touch on politics to find out how he had acclimatised himself to our mode of living, he had, however, his standard reply ready: that he is not a politician but a non-political Naval diver. Knowing his background, this would fit in with his past way of thinking, but I cannot say for certain whether he replies in this way to camouflage his true thoughts.

At present he is definitely not trying to attempt an escape. Having taken the necessary precautions, of course unbeknown to him, I twice gave him the opportunity of disappearing while I left him alone —the first time for 24 minutes, the next time for an hour. But on neither of these occasions did he move at all.

He expressed his appreciation when he found that we were travelling to Leningrad in a sleeper, and also praised his food—especially on the train. He also said that he was grateful to me for driving him about in Leningrad so that he could have a glimpse of this beautiful city before going to the Naval Training Command in Kronstadt.

When I handed him over to the reception officer at the Naval Training Command at 11.34 hours, he thanked me for the good time I had given him, and asked me to repeat his thanks for everything to Col. Myaskov when I next see him.

Signed: Capt. L. B. Chuikov.
Report read: Col. A. F. Myaskov.

REPORT FROM CAPTAIN NIKOLAI PETROVICH KHORNEI-CHUK, COMMANDANT OF THE NAVAL TRAINING COMMAND, KRONSTADT

Saturday, September 1, 1956. 14.00 hours.

Lev Lvovich Korablov reported for duty at 11.34 hours on August 18, 1956, and was immediately attached to the frogman squadron of the Training Command. As I had received the most satisfactory report from his commanding officer on August 20, I promoted Korablov to the function of frogman instructor, to make the best possible use of his abilities and experience.

L. L. Korablov is a highly skilled frogman and a valuable contribution to the command. He takes his duties seriously, works hard and to our full satisfaction, and is most particular in the training of new would-be frogmen.

In his free time he takes part in the usual social activities. He is friendly with everyone but has not yet made a real friend. Though everyone speaks highly of him and appreciates his ready help to anyone who needs his assistance, everybody feels that he keeps strictly to himself and does not wish to disclose his true self.

He has now joined the political schooling course and is reported to be a satisfactory pupil. But, despite his paying the fullest attention to the lectures, he takes part in political discussions in the club only when he feels that he has no other alternative. But even then it is obvious that he is extremely cautious and that he thinks twice before speaking.

Due to the special circumstances and the difficulty in reading Korablov's mind, it is recommended that for the time being he should remain at his present assignment, notwithstanding the fact that on active service he would be a valuable contribution to any command.

Signed: Captain N. P. Khorneichuk.
Report read: Col. A. F. Myaskov.

REPORT FROM CAPTAIN NIKOLAI PETROVICH KHORNEI-
CHUK, COMMANDANT OF THE NAVAL TRAINING COM-
MAND, KRONSTADT

Sunday, September 16, 1956. 16.45 hours.

Lev Lvovich Korablov continues to take his
duties most seriously and shows good results in
training frogmen whom he teaches to cope with any
underwater task. He is pleasant and friendly and is
well liked by officers and men. He makes fair progress in the political schooling course but still does
not readily take part in discussions in the club and
still appears to weigh each word before speaking.
His conduct is in every respect exemplary.

Signed: Captain N. P. Khorneichuk.

Report read: Col. A. F. Myaskov.

REPORT FROM CAPTAIN NIKOLAI PETROVICH KHORNEI-
CHUK, COMMANDANT OF THE NAVAL TRAINING COM-
MAND, KRONSTADT

Monday, October 1, 1956. 15.25 hours.

Lev Lvovich Korablov continues to give satisfaction in every respect and is one of the best men of
the command. Am satisfied that he can be transferred to Operational Command so that his abilities
and experience can be fully utilised. Also recommend that he be raised to officer's rank as I am convinced he will appreciate recognition of his services.

Signed: Captain N. P. Khorneichuk.

Report read: Col. A. F. Myaskov.

MEMORANDUM FROM INVESTIGATION JUDGE COLONEL
ALEKSEI FEOFILOVICH MYASKOV TO CAPTAIN NIKOLAI
PETROVICH KHORNEICHUK

Khimky, Wednesday, October 10, 1956. 11.00 hours.

Agree with your recommendations and with any
posting which you have in mind for L. L. Korablov.
Advise, however, that you inform the chief security
officer of prospective command about the special
circumstances of the man.

Would suggest that Korablov should first be
raised to petty officer, and not at once upgraded to
the rank of a full officer.

Memo read: Captain N. P. Khorneichuk.

REPORT FROM CAPTAIN NIKOLAI PETROVICH KHORNEI-
CHUK, COMMANDANT OF THE NAVAL TRAINING COM-
MAND, KRONSTADT

Sunday, October 28, 1956. 13.00 hours.

Called Lev Lvovich Korablov and at 11.12 hours
told him that because of his satisfactory services he
had been raised to the rank of petty officer and that he
had been transferred to Operational Command in
Arkhangelsk for active service. Handed over to him
his posting orders and his pay book, which now
bears his rank as petty officer. Korablov showed
genuine thankfulness at having climbed to the rank
of petty officer, thanked me, and expressed his
gladness at having been posted to an operational
command.

Petty Officer L. L. Korablov left the Training

Command, Kronstadt, for Operational Command, Arkhangelsk, by duty car at 13.10 hours.

Signed: Captain N. P. Khorneichuk.

Report read: Col. A. F. Myaskov.

REPORT FROM CHIEF SECURITY OFFICER, OPERA-TIONAL COMMAND, ARKHANGELSK, COMMANDER YURIY PAVLOVICH ARAMESHVILI

Wednesday, November 21, 1956. 16.30 hours.

Petty Officer L. L. Korablov has twice been engaged in underwater operational work, and in one instance rendered valuable help to an icebreaker in trouble. These operations were carried out under extremely difficult conditions.

Though the operation was known to be most dangerous, Korablov and others at once volunteered to assist the icebreaker. His courage and success earned him great admiration and praise from almost every officer and man of the Command. The Command recommends his promotion to second lieutenant when the time for promotion is considered opportune.

As to his private life, there is little to say. He is friendly and is liked by everyone, but is happiest alone. He made a close friendship with Radio Officer Sonia Grigoryevna Lipskaya and seems to be very fond of her. But even when alone with her, never speaks about his past and spins a plausible yarn: he has invented the tale that he has had a serious accident which has robbed him of all remembrance of his former life.

Politically he is continuing to make progress. He

attends the political classes punctually and is considered one of the best pupils. But there is still a considerable lack in his political discussion activities, and when finally dared to talk he clearly thinks twice before he speaks. This, of course, might be due to his still limited command of the richness of the Russian language—in every-day conversation, however, his knowledge of the Russian language is no worse than that of any Russian—but it may also be proof that at heart he is still a capitalist-minded element. My allowing for such a possibility may, however, be wrong, and taking into account service, conduct, etc., of the man and firmly believing that regular signs of appreciation and promotions will gradually turn him into one of the best reliable Soviet citizens, I am of the opinion that promoting Korablov to second lieutenant is fully justified.

Signed: Commander Yuriy Pavlovich Arameshvili.

(This report shows the remark):

Promotion proposition accepted, advised respective department accordingly.

Signed: Col. A. F. Myaskov.

REPORT FROM CHIEF SECURITY OFFICER, OPERATIONAL COMMAND, ARKHANGELSK, COMMANDER YURIY PAVLOVICH ARAMESHVILI

Friday, December 28, 1956. 11.30 hours.

This morning received orders from commandant's office to inform Petty Officer Lev Lvovich Korablov that he is included in the promotion list and has been raised to the rank of second lieutenant. At 10.15 hours called Korablov to my office and informed him that, due to satisfactory conduct and special services rendered, he had been promoted full officer and that his promotion to second lieutenant was contained in the Orders of the Day. When told, Korablov stood speechless for a few seconds, blood shot into his cheeks, and then he said: "Thanks, tovarich Commander, thanks very much indeed."

The way L. L. Korablov reacted confirmed that any recommendation was absolutely justified and right, and that the decision to treat him in exactly the same way as any Russian without a past is bound to reap rich rewards.

Signed: Commander Y. P. Arameshvili.

Report read: Col. A. F. Myaskov.

(The *dossier* now contains reports from chief security officer of the Operational Command, Arkhangelsk, Commander Yuriy Pavlovich Arameshvili, dated January 18, February 8, March 1 and March 20, 1957. These reports are short and merely repeat that "Second Lieutenant Lev Lvovich Korablov continues to give most satisfactory service and is always an immediate volunteer for any dangerous or tricky underwater dive. His conduct is exemplary.")

REPORT FROM CHIEF SECURITY OFFICER, OPERA-
TIONAL COMMAND, ARKHANGELSK, COMMANDER YURIY
PAVLOVICH ARAMESHVILI
Sunday, March 31, 1957. 14.45 hours.
This morning received orders from Headquarters

Nord to inform Second Lieutenant Lev Lvovich Korablov that, because of his exemplary service and conduct he has been transferred to Operational Command, Baltiysk, and that his rank had been raised to that of lieutenant. Called Korablov to my office at 13.00 hours and informed him accordingly, handing over to him his posting orders and amended pay book. Korablov thanked me for the promotion and said he had been happy at Operational Command, Arkhangelsk, and that, in a way, he was sorry to leave. When Second Lieutenant Korablov's promotion to lieutenant and posting was made known at 13.10 hours in the Order of the Day, almost everyone in the Operational Command, Arkhangelsk, expressed regret that the well-liked Korablov was leaving.

Lieutenant Lev Lvovich Korablov left Operational Command, Arkhangelsk, by duty car at 13.50 for the aerodrome, from where the aircraft flying to Baltiysk took off at 14.36 hours.

Signed: Commander Y. P. Arameshvili.

Report read: Col. A. F. Myaskov.

REPORT FROM CAPTAIN ALEKSANDR BORISOVICH NIZ-HANSKY, CHIEF SECURITY OFFICER, OPERATIONAL COMMAND, BALTIYSK

Sunday, March 31, 1957. 21.30 hours.

Lieutenant Lev Lvovich Korablov reported for duty at reception office at 21.13 hours, immediately after arrival by air from Operational Command,

Arkhangelsk. Has been attached to frogman duty squadron.

Signed: Capt. A. B. Nizhansky.

Report read: Col. A. F. Myaskov.

REPORT FROM CAPTAIN NIKITA ILYICH MURIANTS, CHIEF
OFFICER, SPECIAL INVESTIGATION BRANCH
Thursday, April 4, 1957. 23.00 hours.

According to orders, I approached Lieut. L. L. Korablov. Pretending not to know his present name, I called him "Buster" and told him that I had met him during the war while serving with the Allies. As ordered, I spoke to him in English, but he said in Russian that he did not understand my language and asked me to repeat to him what I had said in Russian. This I did, but, looking me straight in the eyes, he told me that I must be mistaken as to his identity and that I must have met someone who looked somehow similar to him.

I then mentioned some of the details about him which are contained in the information sheet, watching him closely while I spoke. But not even his eyes betrayed that I was speaking about his past life. Again he insisted that I was mistaken, said he was sorry that I had not found the man I was obviously eager to find, and offered to buy me a drink.

We drank with each other—two rounds of vodka —and I took this opportunity to speak about wartime episodes which are contained in the information sheet. But not once could I discover more than general interest in Korablov's eyes and face. He gave the impression of someone who listens to a stranger telling him something he has not heard before. But he also gave the impression that he was not particularly interested in the subject and was merely listening in order to be sociable.

I am satisfied that it did not occur to him that I acted on instructions and that I had invented my having met him during the war, in order to try to find out to what extent he would talk, should he be found by anyone from his past life. From his behaviour it was clear that he was satisfied with his successful tactics, which must have convinced me that I had mistaken him for someone else.

My having taken Korablov completely unaware and unprepared, and his reaction in such an instance, would lead to the realistic conclusion that L. L. Korablov is fully trustworthy and does not intend to avail himself of any chance to seek protection from any foreign power.

Signed: Capt. N. I. Muriants.

Report read: Most satisfactory. Col. A. F. Myaskov.

MEMO FROM NEWS INFORMATION ROOM, NAVAL INTELLIGENCE STATION, KHIMKY, TO INVESTIGATION JUDGE COL. ALEKSEI FEOFILOVICH MYASKOV

Sunday, May 5, 1957. 11.18 hours.

A message was sent today from London stating that a senior Whitehall officer had stated the following:

"We are satisfied that Commander Crabb did not die when he went into the water at Portsmouth near the Russian warships, here for the visit of Marshal Bulganin and Mr. Khrushchev.

"We have good reason to believe that he was taken aboard one of the ships and is now held in Russia."

The *Tass* correspondent points out:

"This sudden statement of a Whitehall spokesman, published in the British press, indicates that the British Government has not closed the 'Commander Crabb Case' but that further action may be considered at any time."

Memo read: Col. A. F. Myaskov.

REPORT FROM INVESTIGATION JUDGE COLONEL ALEKSEI FEOFILOVICH MYASKOV

Monday, May 6, 1957. 21.00 hours.

Saw memo from news room at 10.02 hours on returning to office for duty after free day. Immediately telephoned Maj. B. M. Smirnov in Leningrad, told him that I consider it imperative to get the body to England at the earliest possible moment and so end for all time the stories of Crabb being alive in the U.S.S.R. Maj. B. M. Smirnov promised to have the body examined at once by experts, and to report their findings to me later in the day.

At 20.43 hours Maj. B. M. Smirnov telephoned me that the body was ready, and his written report on the matter would be despatched to me tonight.

Ordered him to await my further instructions on the matter.

Signed: Col. A. F. Myaskov.

REPORT FROM MAJOR BORIS MARKOVICH SMIRNOV, SPECIAL COMMISSION, STATE SECURITY COMMITTEE

Monday, May 6, 1957. 20.58 hours.

Received telephone call at 10.14 hours from Investigation Judge Col. A. F. Myaskov, informing me of alarming statements in English press about Commander Crabb's being alive in the U.S.S.R. and suggesting that the body be taken to England as soon as possible, to stop these English rumours. I promised to have the body surfaced immediately, and examined by experts. The safety fencing in the area where the body is anchored in the sea was therefore broken down and at 19.52 hours Dr. B. L. Chermak examined the body. His report states:

"At 19.52 hours examined a body in rubber frogman suit and found it decomposed to such an extent that it is most unlikely that any expert would be able to establish the cause of death. I could not, of course, carry out a full post-mortem examination, as Major B. M. Smirnov, who was present, insisted that the frogman's suit must not be opened. But my conclusion about the decomposition of the body has arisen from the fact that after the most thorough examination I was unable to state what had caused the head and both hands to be detached from the body and arms. I am satisfied that no pathologist in the world will be able to establish the cause of death; also that no one can identify the body. The only identifiable parts are the frogman's suit and the flippers, which are still firmly on.

"It appears, however, that the lower part of the

body is better preserved, though this I could not establish for certain as I was not allowed to strip it. My theory of this is based on the following two facts: when examining the body below the waist, I was able to feel its shape through the suit; the second point for my assumption is that below the waistband the body is sealed by a rubber-band which did not permit the sea-water fully to penetrate into the frogman's suit and thus decompose the lower part of the body. But though I assume that the part of the body, from the waist downwards, is in a comparatively good state of preservation, nevertheless I rule out the possibility of its providing sufficient evidence for identification purposes."

I telephoned Investigation Judge Col. A. F. Myaskov at 20.43 hours, and reported to him that the body was ready for his further instructions in the matter, and that I am sending on the doctor's written report to him tonight.

Signed: Maj. B. M. Smirnov.

Report read: Col. A. F. Myaskov.

REPORT FROM INVESTIGATION JUDGE COLONEL ALEKSEI FEOFILOVICH MYASKOV

Tuesday, May 7, 1957. 14.30 hours.

On returning to my office read Maj. B. M. Smirnov's report. Discussed the return of the body with Major-General Maksim Mikhailovich Chuganov, who agreed that it is essential to take the body to England as soon as possible, but he opposed my suggestion of engaging the help of a merchant

162

ship, passing the English coast. He pointed out that
further possible talks in this matter, by Soviet seamen
in foreign ports, must be prevented at the outset. I
agreed and it was mutually decided that this task
should be carried out by a commander of the Red
Navy.

At 12.25 hours, spoke with Commander Vladimir
Ambramovich Shchedrin at Navy Headquarters
about movement of vessels through the Channel.
Commander Shchedrin said that submarines will be
going on a good-will visit to Egypt very shortly, but
the date has not yet been fixed. He undertook to
advise me as soon as all arrangements for the visit are
made.

Telephoned Major B. M. Smirnov in Leningrad,
at 14.15 hours, advised him of the decision to transport the body to England by submarine and ordered
him to have the body ready for transportation at short
notice.

Signed: Col. A. F. Myaskov.

REPORT FROM INVESTIGATION JUDGE COLONEL ALEKSEI
FEOFILOVICH MYASKOV
Friday, May 24, 1957. 11.55 hours.

At 11.17 hours Commander V. A. Shchedrin telephoned and advised me that three submarines would
be leaving base on June 1, 1957, for a good-will visit
to Egypt, and said that Chief Security Officer Captain
Anatol Grigoryevich Muralov, would be on board
the submarine flagship.

Telephoned Major B. M. Smirnov in Leningrad

at 11.32 hours, and instructed him to arrange the safe transport of the body to England with Captain Muralov.

Signed: Col. A. F. Myaskov.

REPORT FROM MAJOR BORIS MARKOVICH SMIRNOV, SPECIAL COMMISSION, STATE SECURITY COMMITTEE

Friday, May 24, 1957. 15 40 hours.

At 11.32 hours received telephone call from Investigation Judge Col. A. F. Myaskov, advising me that three submarines would be leaving base for Egypt on June 1, and ordered me to make the necessary arrangements for the transport of the body to England with Chief Security Officer Captain Anatol Grigoryevich Muralov.

Telephoned Security Command at 11.43 hours, but was informed that Captain A. G. Muralov is off duty until 13.00 hours, when he will communicate with me. At 13.11 hours Captain A. G. Muralov telephoned me. Informed him of the special mission and received his instruction to make arrangements for the body to be alongside the submarine flagship at base on June 1, 1957, at 01.00 hours.

Instructed Lieutenant S. N. Ignatov at 15.25 hours to take over the execution of the operation and ordered him to advise me about the handing-over of the body to Captain A. G. Muralov alongside the submarine flagship at base.

Signed: Major B. M. Smirnov.

Report read: Col. A. F. Myaskov.

REPORT FROM MAJOR BORIS MARKOVICH SMIRNOV,
SPECIAL COMMISSION, STATE SECURITY COMMITTEE
Saturday, June 1, 1957. 02.30 hours.

At 12.30 hours on May 31, 1957, Lieutenant S. N. Ignatov reported that the body was ready for safe transportation to the submarine base. Sanctioned Lieutenant Ignatov's preparations, and ordered him to report to me as soon as he has executed his mission.

At 17.25 hours spoke by telephone to chief security officer, Captain A. G. Muralov; informed him that Lieutenant S. N. Ignatov would hand over the body to him alongside submarine flagship at 01.00 hours on June 1, 1957, and again repeated the special instructions for the execution of the secret mission.

At 02.14 hours, Lieutenant S. N. Ignatov reported to me by telephone that at 01.00 hours he handed over the body alongside the submarine flagship at base to chief security officer of the Submarine Squadron, Captain Anatol Grigoryevich Muralov. The body was secured by steel ropes round the feet and towed in the sea at a safe distance from the submarine flagship, in order that it should remain continuously in the water during the journey.

Signed: Maj. B. M. Smirnov.
Report read: Col. A. F. Myaskov.

REPORT FROM MAJOR BORIS MARKOVICH SMIRNOV,
SPECIAL COMMAND, STATE SECURITY COMMITTEE
Thursday, June 6, 1957. 09.30 hours.

At 00.31 hours submarine headquarters reported that on June 5, at 23.40 hours, they received a coded

radio message from Chief Security Officer Captain
A. G. Muralov, on board submarine flagship, stating:

"ACCORDING TO OUR DETAILED CHARTS WE ARE
APPROACHING SPOT WHERE THE TIDE IS MOST
LIKELY TO WASH CHARGE ASHORE NEAR PORTS-
MOUTH—PODKOM"

On June 6, 1957, at 01.26 hours, submarine headquarters reported receipt of second coded message
from Chief Security Officer Captain A. G. Muralov,
on board the submarine flagship, stating:

"CARGO DESPATCHED 0059 HOURS STOP CHARTS
AND CURRENTS INDICATE THAT ARRIVAL CAN BE
EXPECTED IN 48 HOURS—PODKOM"

Signed: Maj. B. M. Smirnov.
Report read: Col. A. F. Myaskov.

(The *dossier* then records reports from England
which state that "on June 9, 1957, a headless and
handless body of a man in a frogman's suit was
washed up in Chichester Harbour—some 10 miles
from Portsmouth", that "a director of Khainke & Co.,
the firm which used to supply Commander Crabb
with his frogman suits, identified the Pirelli two-
piece suit, in which the body was washed ashore, as
the suit which Commander Crabb had bought from
them and worn", and that a "faded red-and-white
'pirate' shirt, as well as other clothing found on the
body, were identified as those which Commander
Crabb wore on the morning of his disappearance".
These, and other British newspaper reports on the
matter, are followed by the newspaper report which

records the findings of Dr. Donald Plimsoll King, the pathologist who carried out the *post mortem* of the body, and his statement that he could find no clues as to the cause of death. The *dossier* also records the report that, despite Mrs. Crabb being unable to identify the body as that of her husband, the coroner, Mr. G. F. L. Bridgman, nevertheless found that the body was that of Commander Crabb.)

(The next record in the *dossier* is one single sentence and reads: "The body, which was officially identified as that of Commander Lionel Crabb, was cleared by the coroner and buried at Portsmouth on July 5, 1957.")

REPORT FROM CAPTAIN ALEKSANDR BORISOVICH NIZHANSKY, CHIEF SECURITY OFFICER, OPERATIONAL COMMAND, BALTIYSK

Called Lieutenant Lev Lvovich Korablov to my office at 09.15 hours and informed him that "he" was buried on July 5, at the cemetery in Portsmouth. Let him read the English newspapers, which I had received this morning from the press division. Korablov studied most carefully the various newspaper reports in all the English papers and took his time. Not once did he make a remark. But he was smoking heavily. When he finally handed back to me the bundle of newspapers at 11.50 hours, I asked him:

"What do you say to this?" After some considerable pause he replied: "That puts an end to the whole affair." I then told him that we had kept our word to do everything we had promised for him and he acknowledged that was so. From the way he behaved, I am satisfied that he is glad that his past is dead and that from now on only Lieutenant Lev Lvovich Korablov lives.

Signed: Captain A. B. Nizhansky.

Report read: Col. A. F. Myaskov.

★   ★   ★

(Such is the end of the "Commander Crabb Case" *dossier*. The document which the Soviet Secret Service made available to the heads of the State Security headquarters in all the Iron Curtain countries contains, however, the following postscript).
In the additional *dossier*, which is merely entitled "L. L. Korablov", regular monthly reports from the various chief security officers of the Operational Commands in question are contained. As these reports deal only with L. L. Korablov's conduct and service, it is unnecessary to quote them in full, as they are of no special value to heads of State Security headquarters, because no more than is common knowledge could be learned from them.

In order to show, however, that the tactics used by the brilliant brains of the Soviet security officers, concerned in the case of Commander Crabb, were not only ingenious examples of perfect tactics, but that they also prove that a flexible approach to individual cases can show excellent results, it is added that Lieutenant Lev Lvovich Korablov was transferred from Operational Command, Baltiysk, to Operational Command, Odessa, on March 26, 1958. From Operational Command, Odessa, he was transferred in January, 1959, to Operational Command, Sevastopol. On recommendation of Chief Security Officer, Commander Ivan Aleksandrovich Purtsov, Lieutenant Lev Lvovich Korablov was raised to the rank of First Lieutenant on August 31, 1959. On September 7, 1959, he was transferred to the Far Eastern Naval Command, Vladivostok, because this Operational Command urgently requested "highly skilled frogman-divers with vast experience."

(End of the Soviet secret *dossier*.)

IV

WHAT NEXT?

Because of the ruling at the conference of all the heads of State Security Forces of the Iron Curtain countries, held behind closed doors in Moscow from August 3 to 10, 1959, that the Secret Police headquarters of all the countries of the "People's Democracies" should receive "translations of those secret Soviet *dossiers* which might help the foreign comrades of the State Security headquarters to learn from the experience of our best trained investigation judges how to go about in seemingly hopeless cases, and what methods and tactics to apply to break down the prisoner without the application of drugs, violence, or other such methods", and thanks to those heroic secret agents who smuggled the *dossier* out from behind the Iron Curtain, the mystery of what happened to Commander Lionel "Buster" Crabb since he mysteriously disappeared in Portsmouth Harbour on April 19, 1956, has been solved. But the following, perhaps equally puzzling question, still remains unanswered:

Will Investigation Judge Colonel Aleksei Feofilovich Myaskov, or his possible successor, keep the promise which was given to Crabb, to allow him to leave Russia after he has completed his ten-years' service in the Red Navy, and let him return to England?

Though no one can answer this question now, and though the final answer will be given by none other than the Russians themselves at the end of "Lev Lvovich Korablov's" service in the Red Navy—in the Summer of 1966, the strong indication is, that "Buster" Crabb will *never* see his relatives, his friends, and his native country again. The reason for this prediction is not merely arrived at after the fact that *the Russian Secret Police never allows anyone once caught in their net to get out of their clutches*— a fact which anyone can ascertain by studying their practices. The main reason for doubting that Crabb will ever be allowed to leave Russia is:

From the beginning, the Russians stated that a frogman had been seen near their warships in Portsmouth Harbour, but they made it clear at the same time that they had taken *no* action, and that they were quite satisfied with having delivered their Diplomatic

Note to the British Foreign Office. Though deploring the fact that a frogman was sent to carry out an underwater examination of their cruiser, the Russian press nevertheless accepted the British note of apology. Later—as is seen from the Russian Secret *Dossier* and from newspaper reports throughout the world—versions of how Commander Crabb was killed were made known. Though two different versions were put out of how the frogman met his death, no one outside Russia seems to have noted this vital contradiction, and Investigation Judge Colonel Aleksei Feofilovich Myaskov, consequently scored the success he had aimed at.

Taking all this into account, it seems almost impossible for Russia ever to allow Crabb to re-appear anywhere in his own identity. Because, if ever he emerged as Commander Lionel Crabb, the Russians would clearly admit that their official statements about his death, etc., were deliberate lies. Apart from this, there might always be the possibility that he would publicly disclose every detail of what had happened to him, from the moment he was captured by them—a thing which the Soviets can never allow to happen.

This conclusion of course leads to another equally important question:

What will happen to Crabb when his ten-years' compulsory service with the Red Navy is at an end? At the age of 56, will they still expect him to carry out difficult underwater jobs? Will he then be faced with the pitiable fate of having to live to the end of his days in some well-guarded camp—perhaps in Siberia or the Arctic Circle, or would his captors go so far as to have him "rubbed out", if he is of no further value to them?

The answer to this—though merely based on close inside knowledge about Russian methods and tactics —would be:

It is unlikely that after the expiration of Crabb's ten-years' service in the Red Navy he would "disappear without trace". Though it is true that at an age of 56 years he will no longer be able to carry out such underwater work as the Secret Soviet *Dossier* mentions, and though the Russians mean every single word of their slogan "He who does not work need not eat", it is nevertheless most likely that in 1966 First-Lieutenant or possibly even Commander "Lev Lvovich Korablov" will be requested to sign on for another ten years' service in the Red Navy so as to be continuously under safe supervision. This would not necessarily be mere "gratefulness" towards Crabb for his good services; it would, doubtless, be governed by the fact that Crabb is one of the best underwater experts, and although no longer able to undertake all he did in earlier years, he would still be a most valuable adviser and instructor on any difficult subject. Also, having completed his second ten-years' service, he would be at the qualifying age for retirement and —by that time probably having accustomed himself to Soviet life, and having been away for so long, from his relatives, friends, and his native country, he may perhaps no longer wish to return and stir up his, by then, long-forgotten past.

There is, however, still another possibility: the

publication of the Soviet Secret *Dossier,* which found
its way out from behind the close guarded Iron
Curtain and which, despite all Soviet safety precautions, reveals to the world what really happened
to Commander Crabb, may force the Russians to
come out in the open and to produce him, as they have
produced other vanished people in the past. But such
a possibility seems more than unrealistic. Judging
from the close study of Soviet "flexible" methods and
tactics, Russia is more likely to ignore any possible
approaches on the subject—even possible diplomatic
moves—and, in a way, copy the replies which the
British Admiralty and Prime Minister gave at the
time of the disappearance and also state that they have
nothing more to say in the matter. Such a "way out"
would naturally put up a strong "brick wall" and
would make any further attempt impossible to get
anything officially admitted by Moscow.

So, for the time being at least, everything would
point to the sad fact that as far as Russia is concerned,
Commander Crabb will continue to be dead.

The Soviet Secret *Dossier,* besides making most
interesting reading, disclosing not only the "flexible"
methods and tactics which are practised in Russia,
and divulging what actually happened to Commander
Crabb, raises some other important questions, the
answers to which are not contained in the secret document. These are:

What made Crabb suddenly change his mind and
agree to join the Red Navy instead of choosing to be
killed on the spot as a spy?

Under normal circumstances the answer to this

would be very simple: the mere reason of self-preservation—the most natural reason to man. But in his case this self-preservation theory does not quite fit. It must be remembered that the Soviet Secret *Dossier* discloses that Crabb would not admit to any suggestion of having spied for United States Naval Intelligence, though his interrogators threatened that he would be "rubbed out" if he did not co-operate.

He refused food and drink, apparently determined to end his life in preference to being forced through "truth" drugs to give away any naval secrets which were known to him from his underwater jobs, carried out prior to his fatal capture.

When seriously threatened by Investigation Judge Col. Myaskov, he replied: "Drug me if you wish. Shoot me if you wish. But you can't persuade me to betray my country."

Contrary to his heroic behaviour up till then, he unexpectedly not only agreed to join the Red Navy for a period of ten years, but he also distinguished himself with "exemplary service and conduct".

Though we do not know what was going on in Commander Crabb's brain, there is nevertheless a plausible explanation for his "strange" and "contradictory" decision.

The Soviet Secret *Dossier* reveals that Crabb was, from the beginning, threatened that he would be injected with a "truth" drug, with most unpleasant treatment, and even with death, if he did not co-operate. Though he *did not* co-operate, he was neither injected, nor killed. On the contrary. When he showed signs of food-poisoning and general collapse, he received medical treatment. Yet, he had not complied with any of his interrogators' demands but had instead openly defied them all the time. Then, after a period of recuperation, the new investigation judge, Col. Myaskov, suddenly resumed his threats. . . .

Taking into consideration Commander Crabb's unique ability to face up to any unexpected situation most skilfully, it would appear that he was convinced that his captors did not intend to kill him, and that their threats were nothing but attempts to frighten him, so that he would gradually succumb to their requests. This conclusion is mainly arrived at from Commander Crabb's reply to his interrogator as to why the threats had not been carried out already? Consequently, assuming that this theory is correct, he did not risk much when he continued his line of defiance, and when he clearly showed that he was unafraid of ill-treatment and death. By that time he was doubtless aware that his consistent refusal to "co-operate" had earned him admiration not only from his prison guards but also from those who actually held his life in their hands. And the Soviet Secret *Dossier* proved that Commander Crabb's bluff-tactics to be likened to a poker player earned him complete success.

All this gives, of course, only a possible explanation of Commander Crabb's assumed way of thinking while in the hands of the Russian interrogators. But it does not answer the question why he suddenly agreed to join the Red Navy and why all the reports from the various Red Navy commands state that his service and conduct is "exemplary". Though many far-fetched theories for this unexpected decision, etc., could be brought forward, the real answer to this can be given by none other than Commander Lionel Kenneth Philip "Buster" Crabb, O.B.E., G.M., R.N.V.R., himself.

*   *   *

POSTSCRIPT

While this book was in an advanced stage of production, conspicuous headlines CRABB ALIVE—CRABB WORKS FOR RUSSIA — CRABB DOSSIER SECRETS—THE NEW MYSTERY OF BUSTER CRABB, etc., appeared in the British, American and other newspapers of the free world. These informed their readers that this book claims to give the answer to the four-year-old mystery. In Russia and her satellite countries, however, the entire Press and radio network were ordered to maintain complete silence and ignore what was being published abroad. The only exception made was in an *English*-speaking broadcast from Moscow, which said that "anyone believing that Commander Crabb is alive in Russia must be looking through a cracked mirror".

Reports from the Red part of the globe which by-passed the Iron Curtain censors and reached England while this book was in the press, divulge that despite the most stringent orders to all newspapers and radio networks "to ignore the Crabb affair", the Russian Secret Police by no means did so. Far from it. A most concentrated and ruthless investigation into the matter was immediately put into operation—Russian security bosses were determined to discover where and when the leakage occurred.

Men and women who have direct access to secret dossiers *of any sort, were brought before most experienced interrogators and were thoroughly grilled for days on end.* But, after days and nights of third-degree questioning they were, for the time being, released. Each of them has been, however, given to understand that he or she may be arrested at any time and tried for having been party to the treacherous leak.

Reports from behind the Iron Curtain also state that up till now* the Russian Secret Police, Naval Intelligence Officers, and the remaining investigators, have concentrated on discovering whether the leak occurred in Moscow or another Iron Curtain State Security Headquarters. They still do not know from which specific country the secret *dossier* had been smuggled out to England. They will know, of course, when this book is published, and when they see the photographs of the actual pages from the secret *dossier* they will doubtless concentrate with ruthlessness on the State Security Headquarters of the German Democratic Republic.

Though Colonel Myaskov and his fellow inquisitors will have an important lead, they will, nevertheless, have no easy task for, let it be known, that those heroic informants behind the Iron Curtain who supply the free western world with authentic and extremely important documentary evidence of what is going on in the most secret quarters of the Soviets, are *not* the people who have direct access to Secret Police *Dossiers*—they are people who managed to

* Mid-March, 1960.

"borrow" a "spare" copy of the official Moscow translation.

In order to frighten off others and thus try to prevent any possible leakage of a similar nature in the future, the Russian inquisitors might pounce on some innocent victims who have had nothing whatever to do with the matter. But if this happens, it is a risk anyone takes who works in a higher or lower rank of the Soviet Secret Police, and it is well known to them —as well as to anyone who studies the history of the Russian Secret Service—that either real "traitors" or innocent scapegoats of any rank quite frequently disappear without a trace, if "solutions" have to be found.

In England, the Press reports resulted in Members of Parliament questioning the Foreign Secretary, Mr. Selwyn Lloyd, on February 17, 1960, in the House of Commons, about Commander Crabb.* Dame Irene Ward asked the Secretary of State for Foreign Affairs what recent information he has received regarding the whereabouts of Commander Crabb. Mr. Awbery asked the Secretary of State for Foreign Affairs if he will make a statement on the most recent information received by Her Majesty's Government about Commander Crabb.

Mr. Selwyn Lloyd: "No recent information about Commander Crabb has been received by Her Majesty's Government."

Dame Irene Ward: "Can my right hon. and learned Friend give us a little more assurance, having regard to some wild statements which have appeared in the Press and the disquiet which some of those observations have aroused?

* *Hansard*, p. 1259, Volume 617, No. 58.

Has he not got any further statement to make on the subject, on whether we know definitely what happened, and whether there has been identification of the body?"

Mr. Lloyd: "I would remind my hon. Friend that at the inquest in June, 1957, the coroner expressed himself as quite satisfied that the remains which were found in Chichester Harbour on June 9 were those of Commander Crabb."

Mr. Awbery: "Is the Foreign Secretary aware that there is a possibility that the coroner was wrong on that occasion? Is he aware also that a book is being published shortly by publishers in London who state that they are satisfied with the authenticity of the information received from Russia? They are publishing this. Could the Foreign Secretary give us some information about the publication of this book?"

Mr. Lloyd: "I do not know about the book. I have no other information about Commander Crabb than that which I have given to the House. I have no reason to think that there is any truth in the suggestion that the coroner was wrong."

Mr. Fernyhough: "Has not the time come when the Government should come clean with the House about this case, and ought not the House to know who was responsible for giving the instructions to undertake that rather shady escapade?"

Mr. Lloyd: "That is quite a different matter from the two Questions on the Paper."

Next day:*

Commander Kerans asked the the Secretary of State for Foreign Affairs if he will make a statement on the most recent information he has concerning Commander Crabb.

Mr. R. Allan: "I have nothing to add to my right hon. and learned Friend's reply yesterday."

Without criticising Mr. Lloyd for having continued on the same lines which were taken by the then Prime Minister, Sir Anthony Eden, on May 9, 1956,†

* *Hansard*, p. 153, Volume 617, No. 59.
† pp. 12, 13, 14, and 15.

and on May 14, 1956,* his replies that he did not know anything about a book which claimed Crabb was alive in Russia, and that he had no reason to doubt that the coroner was right are, however, answers of a man who has no knowledge of the Soviet Secret *dossier*. But, unless it is decided to continue the policy which was started four years ago, the publication of the authentic Russian version of what really happened to Commander Crabb, together with an investigation into the striking contradictions in the findings before and during the inquest, may possibly result in entirely new developments taking place.

Unfortunately the CRABB ALIVE Press reports came out too early. Had—as is clearly impressed upon the Iron Curtain informants—the Russian Secret Police not been alerted in time, better and more photographic evidence about Commander Lionel "Buster" Crabb, *alias* First-Lieutenant Lev Lvovich Korablov, serving in the Red Navy, could have been smuggled out to England—in time for the publication of this book. This, of course, is now impossible, because the Russian Secret Police have most efficiently clamped down on anything that has the slightest connection with the Crabb-Korablov affair.

Yet, even in its present form, the factual material presented to the reader on the foregoing pages of this book gives authenticity to what happened to the frogman, since he disappeared mysteriously in Portsmouth on April 19, 1956.

* pp. 20, 21, 22, and 23.